TO:

FROM:

Beyond
Copyright © 2007 by Christianity Today International
ISBN 978-0-310-81445-0

Requests for information should be addressed to:
Inspirio, the gift group of Zondervan
Grand Rapids, Michigan 49530
www.inspiriogifts.com

Compiler: Phyllis Ten Elshof
Product Manager: Kim Zeilstra
Design Manager: Michael J. Williams
Production Manager: Matt Nolan
Design: studiogearbox.com
Cover image: Corbis

Printed in China
07 08 09/ 5 4 3 2 1

::Beyond

A Devotional Magazine for Young Women

Contents

HeadTurner

A woman with the latest hairstyles, cosmetics, or skin care can never compete or compare with the loveliness of a woman who has allowed Jesus to occupy every place in her heart. Sure, many women can make heads turn. But do they do the same for hearts?

A woman may walk confidently in a bikini but never know the power of being clothed with the glory of God. She may possess charm but lack grace. Carry a huge workload but never carry a candle to light the world. Run a household but never run to God. It's all vanity. It's all worthless without him.

I yearn to be a woman after Jesus' heart. A woman of faith and grace. A woman who possesses so much of Jesus that people would believe he exists because they recognize his power in me. I want to be a woman who immediately follows every request of my Lord. I desire him. I want to be beautiful in him. Is there any other lasting beauty?

I think of Mother Teresa. What a beautiful soul. What a glory to God. She spread his fragrance to the world. Was it Giorgio? Givenchy? Estee Lauder? No, it was Jesus. Jesus was so evident in her; his life so undeniable; his love so obvious.

But we don't have to be Mother Teresa to impact our world. We don't have to be a tiny nun from Calcutta, India, to represent true humility, servanthood, and compassion. All we have to be is a woman after God's heart.

One of my favorite verses is Psalm 34:5, "Those who look to him are radiant; their faces are never covered with shame." Those who look to Jesus are radiant. Their countenance is that of a thousand stars.[1]

Charm is deceptive, and beauty is fleeting;
    but a woman who fears the Lord is to be praised.

Proverbs 31:30

looking good

Feeling good about how we look is a huge boost to our confidence and gives us a better chance of interacting positively with those we meet every day.

A healthy perspective on inner and outer beauty should be the goal of every believer, says Constance Rhodes, author of Life Inside the Thin Cage and founder of FINDINGbalance (www.findingbalance.com), a ministry that helps people with eating disorders and self-image issues. There's nothing wrong with taking care of our bodies and wanting to look good, she says.

"Feeling good about how we look is a huge boost to our confidence and gives us a better chance of interacting positively with those we meet every day. But when our life begins to revolve around protecting our outward image, then we have crossed the line of allowing our image to dictate how we live our lives. And when this happens, what others think of us becomes more important than what God thinks, which is the true defining line."

Rhodes encourages people to embrace their inner beauty, which she believes begins with recognizing the frailty of outer beauty. "Any of us can spend time, money, and energy to achieve what we consider to be an attractive outer beauty, but we have no guarantee that our investment will pay off," she says. "In fact, we are virtually guaranteed the opposite — all of us will lose much of what our society considers to be outer beauty as we go through the natural aging process of life here on Earth."[2]

Do you not know that your body is a temple of the Holy Spirit, who is in you, whom you have received from God? You are not your own; you were bought at a price. Therefore honor God with your body.

1 Corinthians 6:19–20 NIV

::Loving Your Looks

It is only when we hold physical beauty in high esteem as the handiwork of God that we can fully grieve when people debase it with pride. It's only when we understand how much our brothers and sisters need to believe in their beauty that we can grasp what a crime it is to make them feel ashamed of their inability to pay for the right clothes, or ashamed that God gave them a body shape, bone structure, or skin color that isn't quite good enough. It's only when we confess that we were never meant to suffer aging and death that we can honor youth's glory cleanly and let it go.

The truth is, beauty matters. A 1995 study found that 48 percent of American women felt "wholesale displeasure" about their bodies. That is, about half utterly detested their looks, while many more merely disliked their busts or thighs. This self-hatred has spiraled up from 23 percent in 1972 to 38 percent in 1985.

Men still lag behind women in self-contempt, but discontent is growing both among middle-aged boomers and young men. These people do not need to be told they are vain. They need to be loved, body and soul, until they can look in the mirror and see the image of God.

God didn't tell Leah to stop whining about losing a man's heart to pretty Rachel. The Bible says, "When the LORD saw that Leah was not loved, he opened her womb, but Rachel was barren" (Genesis 29:31 NIV). The world is full of people who are undervalued because of the way they look, and when we care for them as though that pain matters, we affirm their value.

In an address to the Evangelical Christian Publishers Association, a nationally known speaker joked that his wife rarely passed a mirror without checking her appearance. He didn't mind, he said, because "she's my glory!" (alluding to 1 Corinthians 11:7 NIV: "the woman is the glory of man").

I don't have a husband who can get up in front of a roomful of people and say, "She's my glory!" But I am grateful to have a God who says that regularly, often through the words of a friend. I never get tired of hearing it.[3]

The truth is, beauty matters. A 1995 study found that 48 percent of American women felt "wholesale displeasure" about their bodies.

food for life

If your motivation for getting yourself and your family to eat right is so everyone can look good by society's standards, you'll find little scriptural support. According to Genesis 1:27 NIV, God created us in his image with no qualifiers regarding physical appearance or body weight.

However, while vanity is no virtue, exercising regularly and adhering to a nutritionally sound diet require discipline and self-control — character traits strongly emphasized in God's Word. So when I saw my family needed to shape up, I tried to keep my family's efforts to eat well in the context of preserving health, not enhancing appearance.

For starters, I realized that most of us — adults and children — fall short of the U.S. Department of Agriculture's recommendation to eat at least five servings of fruits and vegetables per day. So even though I'd always kept fruit available for snacking and tried to serve a wide variety of vegetables with meals, I needed to go a step further. I started teaching my daughter about the connection between our diet and our health. Choosing food wisely is only half the equation; practicing moderation is the other half. Too much of even the most nutritionally sound food is not a good thing.

Then there's modeling: We can't ask our kids to snack on fruit and yogurt while we eat chips and dip. We can't expect them to be more active if we take the elevator up a single flight of stairs.

I was guilty of not practicing what I preached when it came to fast food. I had set limits on how often we ate out until I had my fourth child. Her birth gave me a convenient excuse for yielding to the temptation of the ubiquitous drive-thru lane. I felt justified because we were such a busy family — surely if anyone was entitled to a quick meal every now and then, we were.

But my excuse was lame, at best. I knew how to prepare quick and healthy meals, and I'd mastered the technique of cooking ahead and freezing for later. What I lacked was discipline. Once I acknowledged the problem, I broke the fast-food habit and went back to my kitchen. And my decision to set a good example led to a double blessing: My family has healthier meals, and my daughter is learning how to cook![4]

30 Lbs.

15 Lbs.   5 Lbs.

Strength Training

Does God care if we lift weights? I believe he does. In 2 Corinthians 7:1 NIV, Paul says, "Let us purify ourselves from everything that contaminates body and spirit, perfecting holiness out of reverence for God."

I believe that when I seek to glorify God in weight lifting, it becomes a holy activity. This act of discipline demonstrates my desire to take good care of the earthly body with which he's entrusted me. That being said, if your to-do list is as long as mine, you're not eager to add one more thing to it.

Here are eight great reasons to add strength training to your busy schedule.

1. You can't afford not to strength train. The reason is simple: As you build muscle and lose fat, your body burns calories more efficiently. You'll burn more calories—even while you're sleeping—and lose weight faster than you would if you did no strength training at all.

2. Increased muscle and decreased fat mean that even if your scale doesn't change, your shape does. Your muscles become firmer and more toned.

3. Lifting weights increases your endurance so everyday activities won't be as taxing.

4. One of your primary weapons against osteoporosis is strength training. Others are a diet rich in calcium and vitamin D and weight-bearing cardiovascular exercise such as walking or jogging.

5. Exercise reverses the trend in the rise of obesity-related illnesses. Strength training helps lower blood pressure and bad cholesterol levels, as well as minimizes some risks associated with type 2 diabetes. It also may help prevent certain types of cancer.

6. Weight training strengthens and tones abdominal and back muscles, making them strong and flexible, thereby decreasing your risk of injury and pain. Strength training can improve your posture in the same way it alleviates lower back pain—by strengthening core muscles. That makes you look thinner and more graceful than you already are.

7. Studies have shown that thirty minutes of exercise a day, three times a week, is as effective as an antidepressant in relieving depression symptoms. While you should consult a physician if you feel depressed, remember that something as simple as exercise may help keep those symptoms at bay.

8. People who exercise fall asleep more quickly, sleep more deeply, awaken less often, and sleep longer than those who don't. And better sleep at night means more energy during the day.[5]

Pampering Yourself

The Spa Girls, Melissa Calvert and Lisa Seale, two working moms in the Houston area, launched their creative women's ministry in 2004 as a way to integrate teaching women inexpensive ways to pamper themselves along with memorable ways of sharing Scripture. (The "Spa" in Spa Girls stands for Spiritual, Practical, and Amusing.)

"We emphasize that a woman's true beauty and self-worth come first and foremost from a personal relationship with Jesus," says Melissa. "So when we talk about lipsticks, we mention verses about the Lord setting a guard on our lips. When we show them how to make their own bath salts, we talk about believers being the salt of the earth. We hope these verses come to mind the next time the women put on their lipstick or soak in a hot bath."

So how can you pamper yourself and save money with common household products? "Did you know that bath salts are basically rock salt, oil, and fragrance?" Me-lissa asks in Spa Cents, one of their presentations. The recipe, one of many they pass out to attendees, calls for one cup of rock salt or Epsom salt; one tablespoon of baby oil, mineral oil, sweet almond oil, glycerin, or olive oil; and any type of scent you enjoy. Place these items in a tightly sealed jar and turn it every few hours for a day or two before using.

You can make your own face mask using Pepto-Bismol or milk of magnesia. Rinsing your hair in mouthwash helps remove product buildup. And you can exfoliate your lips with an old toothbrush ("preferably your own," Lisa jokes) and Vaseline.

The Spa Girls encourage women to take at least one hour each month to pamper themselves. But more than anything, Lisa says, "We want a woman to know God thinks she's beautiful and loves her unconditionally."[6]

The Spa Girls encourage women to take at least one hour each month to pamper themselves.

extreme Weight Loss

After a frightening drop of thirty pounds in three months, the manager of my local gym forbade me to return, my boss ordered an immediate leave-of-absence, and a physician-friend implored my husband, John, to seek medical intervention.

John pleaded with me to get help, so I reluctantly let him take me to a clinic. There the physician weighed me in at seventy-nine pounds.

I felt deeply ashamed to hear what I already knew: "You have anorexia."

It's been four years since that diagnosis. Recovery's been slow, but not elusive. During one dark moment, I recalled a sermon in which my pastor lit a candle to illustrate Isaiah 42:3 NIV: "A bruised reed he will not break, and a smoldering wick he will not snuff out."

"Yes, God," I thought. "You keep my light burning; you still believe in me!" I knew God would heal me if I'd release my need for control to him. When I went to God for help, I found such Bible verses as, "Do not be wise in your own eyes; fear the LORD and shun evil. This will bring health to your body and nourishment to your bones" (Proverbs 3:7, 8 NIV).

I started working with a caring dietician who helped me understand my need for food to cure my malnutrition. She required me to eat a minimal amount of calories—two thousand—and record them in a food diary. At first I exaggerated my calorie count because I was afraid I'd return to overeating.

Breaking down my resistance invoked a lot of prayer. I struggled with fear and shame, and when destroying thoughts came, Do you really need to eat dinner? Remember those four jellybeans from this morning? I quoted James 4:17 NIV, "Anyone, then, who knows the good he ought to do and doesn't do it, sins."

Each day, I had choices: Either follow my fears, perpetuating the struggle, or surrender to God's power and freedom. Even today, I still must consciously choose to follow Christ in every decision.

I'm so thankful Jesus offers his grace, acceptance, and love to everyone—young girl, daughter, wife, mother, career woman—who needs significance, purpose, and understanding. The world urges us to be attractive, profitable, and totally capable in every role. Yet I've discovered that while it's desirable to succeed, God's grace covers our abilities, our needs, and even our shortcomings and failures. I am God's daughter—totally accepted, pleasing, and loved in his sight—just as I am.[7]

When I first became a Christian, I'd hear numerous testimonies of how God had taken the desire to smoke away from other new believers, but I didn't want him to release me yet. I enjoyed what had become my pack-and-a-half-a-day habit so I convinced myself God was okay with my smoking. After all, no Scripture specifically says, "Do not smoke."

relief from smoking

When I first became a Christian, I'd hear numerous testimonies of how God had taken the desire to smoke away from other new believers, but I didn't want him to release me yet. I enjoyed what had become my pack-and-a-half-a-day habit so I convinced myself God was okay with my smoking. After all, no Scripture specifically says, "Do not smoke."

I knew 1 Corinthians 6:19 says our body is the temple of the Holy Spirit, and we should keep it holy. But I didn't want to believe smoking went against this command. According to my thinking, I was taking care of my body: I ate salads and exercised once in a while. Deep down, however, I realized God wasn't buying my rationalization. The words "quit smoking" kept echoing in my head until one day when I became oddly uncomfortable with my habit.

When that day came, I was ready to let go. This time I was willing to let God be in control and take the desire to smoke from me. The urge to smoke didn't leave me right away. I struggled — especially in the first year of my freedom — but God helped me. I relied on Philippians 4:13 TNIV: "I can do all this through him who gives me strength."

In the first few months I drank lots of water to flush out my system and curtail my body's craving for nicotine. I took long walks and prayed throughout the day. My relationship with Christ became more intimate than I dreamed was possible. I came to realize God wasn't pleased that cigarettes satisfied my need for comfort. He wanted to comfort me. He also wanted me to be his servant — not a servant to my addiction.[8]

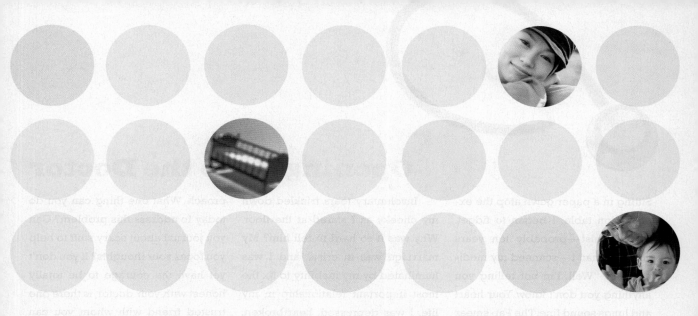

Understanding Baby Blues

A few years ago, I was asked to lead a Bible study at my church. As part of the training, I was required to read a book and watch a video series titled Crisis Care by noted Christian counselor H. Norman Wright. In his book he writes, "If you don't recognize something as a loss, then you don't spend time and energy dealing with it and grieving over it."

When I read that, my eyes watered. I finally understood what I'd gone through emotionally with my depression after my daughter's birth years before.

Until that moment, I never dreamed having a baby was a type of crisis. My parenting books said I'd experience great changes in my life. No one wants to think of having a baby as a loss. My daughter, Jennifer, was a gain. But after reading Wright's book, I discovered that in addition to experiencing fluctuating hormone levels mixed with exhaustion, I was grieving my loss of control, freedom, and former lifestyle. Realizing this allowed me to grieve consciously and continue to move forward with a healthy, hopeful mindset.

Although my bout with postpartum blues resolved itself as time went by, I've wondered what would have happened if my mom hadn't helped me. Looking back, I realize I shouldn't have been embarrassed to discuss my feelings with my doctor. My depression could have gotten worse.

Knowing what I know now, I urge any woman who suspects she might be suffering from depression to seek medical advice as soon as possible. You don't have to display all the symptoms of clinical depression to be considered depressed. Don't be embarrassed that your friends might find out. Don't wait until it gets worse. And if you know someone who might be depressed, urge her to see her doctor—even offer to make the appointment for her and take her there.

When my daughter's grown and perhaps having babies of her own, I know I won't be able to prevent her from going through some of the same difficulties I did. But if she has a similar experience, I pray she'll be able to talk to me about her feelings and I'll be able to help her the way my mom and others helped me. And I hope she'll be able to rely on God for direction, strength, and peace.[9]

Opening Up to the Doctor

Sitting in a paper gown atop the examination table, I began to fidget. My internist—probably ten years younger than I—scanned my medical data. "Well, I'm not telling you anything you don't know. Your heart and lungs sound fine. The Pap smear results will be back in a couple days. Your mammogram looks fine.

"But your cholesterol's up, your weight's creeping up, and the Tagamet apparently isn't helping your stomach troubles. Then there's the insomnia ..." He closed the folder, folded his hands, and looked me in the eye.

"You know, Verla, each of your symptoms has a stress component. Is there anything else you'd like to share about what's going on with you?"

Involuntary tears trickled down my cheeks as I stared at the floor. Why was it so hard to tell him? My marriage was in crisis, and I was humiliated by my inability to fix the most important relationship in my life. I was depressed, heartbroken, and didn't know what to say. As it turned out, I didn't have to. My body announced it for me.

Despite a society willing to tell all on *Oprah* or *Hard Copy*, many women—especially Christians—have a hard time opening up to healthcare professionals committed to their wellness. But, says gynecologist Dr. James Stough, a doctor can't fix our problem if he doesn't know what's really going on.

If you're like me, it's time to face your fears. Take the small-step ap-

proach. What one thing can you do today to address this problem? Can you journal about scary stuff to help you focus your thoughts? If you don't yet have the courage to be totally honest with your doctor, is there one trusted friend with whom you can be truthful? Someone with whom you could role-play what you'd like to say to your doctor?

Then I suggest you forgive yourself. Whether it's guilt for having a medical problem you think you as a Christian should be able to handle, or guilt for keeping it hidden, or denying a serious problem exists, give yourself the same measure of grace God extends to you.[10]

"In him we have ... the forgiveness of sins, in accordance with the riches of God's grace that he lavished on us." No puny forgiveness allowed. Be lavish. That's his model.

Ephesians 1:7-8

Your beauty should not come from outward adornment, such as braided hair and the wearing of gold jewelry and fine clothes. Instead, it should be that of your inner self, the unfading beauty of a gentle and quiet spirit, which is of great worth in God's sight.

1 Peter 3:3-4 NIV

Chapter Two

Growing in God

Happiness His Way

I believe God allowed my injury from my diving accident. This is hard for some people to accept because God is the author of every good thing, and people wonder, "How could quadriplegia be good?"

Too often we try to figure out how God might fit our circumstances into his plan for good, which we think will result in a new job, healing, somebody's salvation, or a husband coming to repentance. But God's driving desire is to rescue us from sin. His goal helps us root out everything that separates us from our ultimate happiness — becoming more like Christ.

We think happiness is found in purchasing that tennis bracelet, getting that second car, redecorating that back bedroom, or losing those extra pounds. Yet Jesus constantly tells us, "Be holy as I am holy." We sing about his holiness on Sunday, but on Monday, how many of us say no to our prideful choices and yes to his way?

I actually have it easy when it comes to this. Sometimes I look at some of my friends who are struggling with obeying God, and I thank him. Because of my disability, I don't have a lot of options. I can't reach for certain pleasures or grasp at something I think might give me happiness. I have no choice but to look to God to meet all my needs.

In his book A Shepherd Looks at Psalm 23, Philip Keller explains that sometimes a shepherd needs to take his rod and splinter a lamb's shin so it can't keep wandering off.

Before my accident, I was that wayward lamb. I was going to purchase my birth control pills, go off to college, sleep with my boyfriend, and do my own thing. Then God took his rod and splintered my shin. The cracking of my shin is a severe mercy. But look where it's landed me — in God's lap! And that's a pretty nice place to be.

The reality is, God wants to give us his joy, but he shares his joy on his terms. Some of those terms call for us to suffer as his Son did to make us more like him.[1]

craving scripture

Feeling good about how we look is a huge boost to our confidence and gives us a better chance of interacting positively with those we meet every day.

After my son's birth, I experienced a prolonged case of "baby blues." Although I found some solace in talking to other moms, journaling, and scheduling me-time, I found the most peace and comfort in God's Word. I found particular reassurance in reading the Psalms — seeing how David cried out in fear, confusion, and even despair but consistently returned to God as his refuge and strength.

At other times, I've turned to Scripture to find direction, wisdom, and encouragement. The Bible holds all this for us, and much more. Psalm 119:105 tells us God's Word is "a lamp to [our] feet and a light for [our] path." Psalm 111:10 reminds us that "the fear of the LORD is the beginning of wisdom; all who follow his precepts have good understanding." Just as physical exercise releases feel-good chemicals in our brains, reading Scripture releases all kinds of spiritual benefits and blessings in our lives, such as increased wisdom, comfort, and peace.

But just as we have different personalities that may require different approaches to reading the Bible, we go through life stages that may demand a change in our Bible reading. A mother of three preschoolers might not be able to devote the same amount of time and energy reading God's Word as a woman whose children are in school.

Take a look at your roles and responsibilities. Make sure you're not trying to do too much or too little for your circumstances. Finding the method of study and reading that works for where you are right now will keep you from giving up in frustration.

I know there will be times when I don't feel such an intense craving for Scripture. But I also know the important thing is for each of us to be aware of our desire for God's Word and be working to increase it.[2]

: :Alone with God

From the time he created us, God knew it would be difficult for us to carry out his commands. In his wisdom he provided the Holy Spirit to enable us do what we can't do on our own. Second Peter 1:3 says that our God and Savior gives us all the tools we need to live a life that pleases Him. So when I struggle spiritually, I remind myself that God doesn't expect me to do it alone. I can rely on the power of the Holy Spirit to give me power over sin.

But to rely on his power effectively, we need to give him time. If you've been struggling to spend time with God, evaluate your schedule. If you're too busy to spend time with God, you're too busy. Don't be afraid to eliminate some activities. The change doesn't need to be drastic. It may be as simple as getting out of bed thirty minutes earlier in the morning, or skipping "The Late Show" so you can have a quiet time before you go to sleep.

Decide where and when it's easiest for you to be alone with God. Make an appointment with him, and treat it like you would an important meeting. If it helps to write this appointment in your day planner, do it.

Depending on your personality, you may like variety and spontaneity in your devotional life, or you may prefer a routine. Whatever you do, find ways to make your quiet time special. Brew a cup of your favorite tea, light a candle, and plug in a CD of Christian music. If you are fortunate enough to have space in your home, create a corner with a comfortable chair, a pretty table, and some potpourri. You'll begin to look forward to your time alone with God, and it'll be easier to make it a priority.[3]

::Giving Up Control

Former child star Lisa Welchel sensed God wanted her to stop making most of the decisions in her marriage and family. "I wanted Steve to be the leader in our home, but God helped me see that I needed to get out of Steve's way so he could lead," she said. So instead of jumping in and making financial, parenting, or time-management decisions for their family, Lisa stepped back for forty days. Every time a decision had to be made, she said to her husband, "Do whatever you think is best, honey."

Was it difficult? "Of course!" Lisa says. "Steve wasn't used to calling the shots for our family. There were times when he made decisions I wouldn't have and when I knew the outcome wouldn't be the best." One decision resulted in losing money, but in that Lisa learned a valuable lesson. "I was reminded how everything we have comes from God. Some of Steve's decisions took us to the bottom. But as a result, I'm not afraid of the bottom anymore. I've learned firsthand that God is there." God also brought good through other decisions Steve made. "Once Steve realized that even when he made bad decisions I wasn't going to leave or say, 'I told you so,' that brought healing to our marriage, Lisa says. "Submitting to him and letting him use his gifts have been such a blessing to our family. I learned there's such freedom in not having to be in control all the time. And I learned that ultimately, I'm not just trusting in my husband, I'm trusting in God."[4]

> In the same way, the gospel is bearing fruit and growing throughout the whole world—just as it has been doing among you since the day you heard it and truly understood God's grace.
>
> Colossians 1:6

Spiritual Grazing

Knock, knock. You've just discovered your grocery coupons have expired, your teen is bringing her boyfriend over, and your two-year-old is happily floating his shoes in the toilet.

Knock, knock. "Who can that be?" you wail, grabbing your toddler before he dives in headfirst. You recognize who is standing at the door. It's Jesus!

"May I come in?" he says. "We'll sit down and eat together."

"I would love to, Lord," you say with a sigh. "But I don't have the time right now. Let's get together when I don't have to work anymore or when the kids get in school. Or when I can afford to get some household help." Sound familiar?

The truth is, intimacy with Jesus Christ cannot wait until the time, place, and situation are perfect. No matter what our age; whether we work outside the home or not; whether we're single, married, with or without children; we all need to connect with God.

If consistent time with God is a struggle, perhaps "grazing" is the answer.

Experts in nutrition tell us eating multiple small meals a day, or grazing, can be healthy. Why not adopt a similar principle in your spiritual eating habits? Choose times, places, and materials for your daily renewal that mesh with your individual lifestyle.[5]

praying as you go>>

We women are busy! Work, kids, church commitments, cooking and cleaning, and a myriad of other things that demand our time each day. If you struggle for time to connect with your Creator, the only one who can really help you with all those things on your to-do list, why not borrow some ideas from other busy woman?

Here's what they say:

I used to get frustrated waiting for my computer to fire up and then to connect to the Internet. It seemed to take forever. But now I find this a perfect time to connect with God through prayer. Wouldn't you know it, the time seems too short now!

— Lisa Hendry, Colorado

I pray during my son's nap-time. I've found it's the most practical time for me in this stage of my life. I've tried to pray early in the morning, but I'm not a morning person. At night, I want to spend time with my husband.

—Julie Potter, Missouri

In addition to regular prayer time at home, I find moments throughout my day to speak to God — walking in my neighborhood, riding my exercise bicycle, driving in my car, sitting in my office before one of the classes I teach, even while cleaning my shower.

—Ruth Aipperspach, Texas

When I'm on the way to work, I turn off the radio and pray about the things preying on my mind. This helps me give all my cares to God before I get caught up in the worries of the day. Also, when I'm in the school drop-off line, I pray with my ten-year-old son about what's happening at school that day. We end the prayer with me placing my hand on his head and blessing him. My son may be too big to kiss me goodbye in front of his friends, but he loves receiving this blessing every morning.

—Ellen Symonds, Alabama

I pray while I walk my dog every morning. I pray for protection for my kids as they head off to school, and for my husband as he puts in another day of work to provide for our family. I thank God for the breathtaking sunrise and an occasional bunny or deer that delight me with God's magnificent creation—reminding me of who's in charge of my life.[6]

— Suzanne L. Barath, Ohio

prayer by email

"God, please guard her heart and mind."
"Thank you, God, for the reminder that YOU keep your promises."

While out for a drive during a season of unbearable financial, emotional, and spiritual strain, I realized something in my life was missing: someone to pray with me regularly.

When I arrived home, I immediately logged on to my computer and composed an email asking Linda to be my e-prayer partner for at least a month. As I clicked "send," my heart filled with anticipation for what daily prayer could do for my current situation.

The next day I received Linda's reply: "Yes, I'll pray with you. Your message was timely. I've been thinking about you and how much I need you."

"Wow, this isn't just for me. It's for Linda, too," I thought. As a pastor's wife, Linda needed a confidante outside her church for prayer and accountability. To show her readiness, she sent the first prayer.

We began to send daily emails, just one- or two-sentence prayers. From sign-on to sign-off, that took less than fifteen minutes. We prayed for specifics: "Please give wisdom in the decision next week." We prayed Scripture: "God, please guard her heart and mind with your peace." We were honest with God: "I'm discouraged today, Lord, and don't know how much longer I can go on." We questioned: "Sometimes you seem far away, Lord." We praised: "Thank you, God, for the reminder that you keep your promises." We spoke to God from our hearts and kept each other's concerns confidential.

God used that initial month of daily emails to quiet my heart in the midst of turmoil. I began to recognize that walking with God in the middle of the woods is more vital than finding a way out. With him, we find stability, rest, and hope, no matter what path we're on.[7]

The Benefit of Forgiveness

We've all needed to forgive someone who hurt or wronged us. This is even harder to do when there's no apology. While there are no easy formulas for forgiveness when you've been wronged, keep these things in mind:

1. Forgiveness is a process, not an event. One woman spent the better part of two years doing the work of forgiveness. She directed tearful tirades and whispered prayers of pain at God. She read Christian authors on the topic. She worked hard at the part she could work on—her mind—and trusted God to work in her heart. With a deep awareness of God's forgiveness of her own sinfulness, she's arrived at a deeply resolved forgiveness for her husband.

2. Forgiveness and reconciliation aren't synonymous. Jesus talks about forgiveness in very different situations, both when there's repentance on the part of the offender (Luke 17:3) and when there isn't (Matthew 18:21). Forgiveness is about what you do, not what the person you're forgiving does. For reconciliation to take place, there has to be work on both ends of the relationship. And in some cases, especially those involving the threat of continued abuse, reconciliation isn't desirable. You can forgive without forgetting.

3. Work for reconciliation. When we feel we've been wronged, especially when sin is involved, we must talk with the offender (Matthew 18:15), if at all possible. Sometimes it's easier to forgive than to have that kind of conversation. But openly facing the issue could bring the clarity necessary for either repentance or for shared responsibility and mutual forgiveness.[8]

Sharing Your Story

Jesus didn't preach a lot of three-point sermons, but he told a ton of stories. Why? People are interested in other people, not abstract ideas. That's why you're reading this and not a philosophy textbook.

Imagine trying to convince the woman next door she's a sinner and desperately needs Christ. Yeah, right! But what if you talk to her about how you overcame trouble in your life through Christ? She may be willing to talk about the Gospel after hearing a sincere personal testimony.

Are you ready to share your story? You may find it helps to write your story and then practice it. Then when you have an opportunity to tell that story to someone, you can do so with confidence. Your story should include three parts:

1. What life was like before knowing Christ. You may want to talk about a specific problem you struggled with.

3. What life is like now. How are you a different person as a result of having Christ in your life? What does he mean to you?

2. How you came to know Christ. Don't just say, "I came to know Christ." Offer details about how it happened.

As you craft your story, remember to keep it brief. Two to five minutes is plenty. But give enough details to arouse interest. Ask God for wisdom and guidance, and trust the Holy Spirit to do his work preparing the recipient's heart.

When sharing your testimony, don't speak "Christianese," such as, "I felt it was God's will" or "Jesus shed his blood for our sins." Talk like that means nothing to unchurched people. Also, don't give the impression that becoming a Christian means becoming problem-free. Be honest and real. Don't be preachy. And don't speak in a judgmental or critical way. Be loving and accepting.

God has an unending supply of creativity; ask him to use your story to help others. Just think of the fun you'll have someday tracking down those people in heaven to discover how your story blended with theirs.[9]

We must patiently persevere, even in suffering, because God wants us to grow stronger in character. Romans 5:3–4 reminds us, "We also glory in our sufferings, because we know that suffering produces perseverance, perseverance, character; and character, hope." Patience in suffering pleases God and teaches us to be more like his Son.

Gifts of Patience

We have heard stories of God performing a miracle in the eleventh hour, when there was no longer any possible human intervention or hope. In those cases, patience results in God being glorified and praised. But sometimes I must endure suffering for reasons only God knows and will reveal to me in heaven, when time is no longer relevant.

In the meantime I wait, trusting that the loving God who created all things and knows all things also knows what is best. When impatience over my parents' unbelief or any other trouble plagues me with sleepless nights and dark days, I fall before God in thankful prayer, claiming his promise in Philippians 4:6–7: "Do not be anxious about anything, but in every situation, by prayer and petition, with thanksgiving, present your requests to God. And the peace of God, which transcends all understanding, will guard your hearts and your minds in Christ Jesus."

Prayer gives me the peace I need to be patient. Even if my parents' seedling never sprouts, my own faith will continue to flower and bloom.[10]

A Church to Call Home

Several years ago, everything at our home church changed. After praying about the situation for three months, my family and I felt prompted to move on. According to the Barna Research Group, one in seven people will look for a new church this year. In case you're among that one in seven, following are some important questions we learned to ask in the search process:

1. Does this church preach God's Word? Look for a place where truth is preached from the Bible; where God's Word is seen as living, relevant, changeless, and inerrant rather than just a good book filled with advice on how to be a more loving, moral person.

2. Does this church provide meaningful worship? The style of worship is usually a matter of taste. But for all our style preferences, it's the message in worship that counts. In itself, exciting music doesn't necessarily draw us into God's presence any more than majestic or brooding music. The purpose of worship isn't to meet a style preference or elicit an emotional response in people; it's to glorify God.

3. Is the church convenient? Your church needs to be close enough for you to become plugged into more than just Sunday services. You need to become active in its programs throughout the week to feel like more than a casual attender.

4. Can you contribute to this church's work? God gives you gifts and talents to build his church. You can tell a church has opportunities for you to serve when the bulletin lists opportunities that match your spiritual gifts and interests. Another good sign is receiving a warm, welcoming invitation from a ministry leader to serve.[11]

We continually ask God to fill you with the knowledge of his will through all the wisdom and understanding that the Spirit gives, so that you may live a life worthy of the Lord and please him in every way: bearing fruit in every good work, growing in the knowledge of God.
Colossians 1:9–10

Jesus promised, "For where two or three come together in my name, there am I with them."
Matthew 18:20

Chapter Three

Rest

The Joy of Rest

Faith allows people to emulate God and rest from their works. Life is too demanding for those of little faith, because the inability to rest is the incapacity to let go of the illusion of control.

The constant need to work, shop, and meet demands can be a practical denial that God is in control. Conversely, a spiritual discipline of regular rest from the constant drive to check items off a to-do list can be a powerful symbol of our trust in God's sufficiency.

Taking time to rest takes planning, because our lives are swept along by the currents of modern culture. Our culture fosters accumulation, which teaches us to value ourselves primarily in economic terms. It even teaches us to rate our leisure by the number and the quality of our toys rather than by the restorative quality of our play. We are also shaped by the kind of thinking that teaches us to justify every activity in terms of its usefulness to us and others.

There is a gratuitous quality to Sabbath rest. It is antithetical to utility. The celebration of the goodness of God and of his creation needs no further justification.

Rest and leisure are from God. And the world can't take them away.[1]

The Lord is my shepherd, I lack nothing.
He makes me lie down in green pastures,
he leads me beside quiet waters,
he refreshes my soul.

Psalm 23:1 – 3

teaching kids rest

In our frantic society in which first-graders are in football leagues and children carry PDAs and Day-Timers to keep up with after-school events, we need, more than ever, to "remember the Sabbath day by keeping it holy" (Exodus 20:8).

Karen-Marie Yust, a mother of three and author of *Real Kids, Real Faith: Practices for Nurturing Children's Spiritual Lives*, says that in this overscheduled and overworked world, kids need to learn that they must take time to rest and focus on God. "Our culture sends us the opposite message — if you're not frantically on top of everything, belonging to every imaginable club, and working all the time, you will be unhappy and unsuccessful," says Yust. But there is real power in taking a rest.

God's commandment to keep the Sabbath holy reminds us that God is in charge and that taking a break is good. It reminds us to say to our kids, "You will get into college even if you don't have that eighth extracurricular activity on your application."

Parents wishing to keep the Sabbath should start slowly. Dorothy Bass in *Receiving the Day: Christian Practices for Opening the Gift of Time*, reminds parents to focus on putting good Sabbath practices in place rather than emphasizing what one can't or shouldn't do on Sunday.

Instead of making Sundays primarily a time when one can't work, make Sunday afternoon a family time for all those restful, enriching activities you don't have time for during the week.

But the Sabbath isn't only about restful family time. There should also be elements of Sabbath observance that draw the family's attention to God. Attending church together, of course, is a good starting point.

Singing a hymn at the beginning or end of a meal can direct us toward our Creator, whose rest we imitate on the Sabbath, and our Redeemer, whose resurrection we celebrate on the Sabbath.[2]

As women, we can easily bring our culture's values into our attempts to observe the Sabbath. We so easily forget the core meaning of the Sabbath — to stop and rest — that we end up turning Sabbath observance into one more thing to achieve.

Loving Sabath Rest

When I was a part-time student and stay-at-home mom, work consisted of studying, housework, and shopping. For my husband, work involved anything from doing his paid job to house repairs and lawn mowing. We didn't do any of those tasks on Sunday.

Today, turning on my computer, balancing my checkbook, weeding my garden, and cooking all qualify as work. But I know some people who find gardening and cooking relaxing; those women have a different list of work activities they avoid to find rest.

Some work from which we need a rest is mental. One woman I know tries to avoid worry on the Sabbath. She considers herself a worrier and feels overwhelmed at the thought of trying not to worry every day. One day a week, however, feels manageable. So she gives herself a day in which not to worry. That has been a great gift to her.

Many women benefit from some silent time on their day of rest. One single woman who works in a people-intensive job spends her Sabbath afternoon alone. Then she often meets up with friends for supper. One mom prepares special activities for her young children to do on Sunday afternoon. During that special hour, her children play alone, enjoying "Sabbath box" activities while their parents get some quiet time.

We want to experience God's presence on the Sabbath, but we need to experiment with unforced ways to do it. As soon as we're working too hard to achieve rest on the Sabbath, we've violated the central idea of the day.[3]

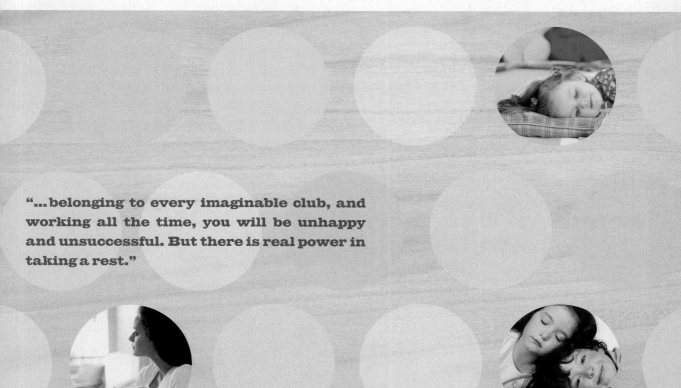

"...belonging to every imaginable club, and working all the time, you will be unhappy and unsuccessful. But there is real power in taking a rest."

ZZZZ

Getting Enough Sleep

The kitchen looked like a war zone. It was 10 a.m., and last night's dirty dishes were still piled on the counter. I was in my bathrobe, my son was in his pajamas, and I didn't have one speck of energy or motivation to handle the five thousand things demanding my attention. As I shuffled along, picking up dishes, I moaned softly to myself, thinking, "Why am I so tired?"

Thankfully, we don't have to drag ourselves through life constantly running on empty. The Bible tells us we can have much more than that. As John 10:10 NIV says, "I have come that they may have life, and have it to the full."

Sleep is essential for rebuilding your body — so stop feeling guilty about insisting on having enough of it. But how much sleep do you really need? Experts say it depends on the person. If you're constantly jerked out of a deep sleep by the alarm, or if you usually feel drowsy during the day, you need more sleep. Try these sleep-friendly habits:

1. Establish a firm bedtime. This practice helps overcome what my husband calls "bedtime inertia," that feeling of being glued to the couch and too tired to get ready for bed. Since our alarm goes off at 5:45 a.m., my husband and I start getting ready for bed at 9:30 p.m., and settle into bed by 10 p.m. A set bedtime also makes it easier to turn off the television, another prime sleep snatcher.

2. Wind down. When I go at it hard all evening, then flop into bed, it's difficult for me to fall asleep, even though I'm exhausted. My mother used to talk about being "too tired to sleep." Now I know what she meant. I've learned I need some time to unwind before I hit the sheets. Sipping a cup of herbal tea or warm milk can soothe frazzled nerves or an over-wired body.

Others find a warm soak in the tub for ten or fifteen minutes before bedtime works wonders. I've been doing the soaking routine for some time now and definitely feel more rested in the morning. Try recording your evening activities for a week — chances are, you'll find things you can eliminate so you can add some needed wind-down time.[4]

After nine months of waiting followed by the intense work of childbirth, the time has finally arrived. You're ready to take your baby home. You look forward to basking in the warmth of your own home.

Resting with a New Baby

You can imagine yourself curling up on the couch after tucking the baby in bed, sparkling cider in your hand.

The fantasy disappears as soon as you walk in the front door. Rather than peacefully sleeping, your baby starts crying. Well-intentioned friends arrive, asking for a peek. Two hours later, with your baby asleep at last, you both collapse, exhausted, on the couch.

With a new baby, life changes substantially, but you can take the following steps to ease this major life transition and get the rest you need:

1. Limit visitors. The "babymoon" is not a time for extensive socializing. Don't feel reluctant to limit phone calls and visitors. Like the honeymoon, the transition period after a baby's birth is a time of bonding and intimacy for mother and baby. Consider setting visiting hours each day for a period of sixty to ninety minutes every evening.

2. Go to bed as soon as you get home. By getting into comfortable pajamas and climbing into bed, you'll be more likely to get the rest you need — and send a message that you're unavailable for work. New moms, even if they have eight children, appreciate time alone with the new baby and time to rest.

3. Pamper yourself. Take at least one long, relaxing shower every day. Revel in back rubs, fresh flowers, and a peaceful atmosphere within the home. A new robe, softly scented body lotion, or a bright-colored cotton sweat suit can make you feel valued. If you are tired, ask your husband to bathe and change the baby while you rest. Or lie down together — just the three of you — to nap.

When the psalmist wrote, "I have stilled and quieted my soul; like a weaned child with its mother," he was describing a contentment and inner quietness that comes from trust. While it may seem you may never again get the rest you need, trust God. Use this opportunity to experience the Lord's ability to supply your needs.[5]

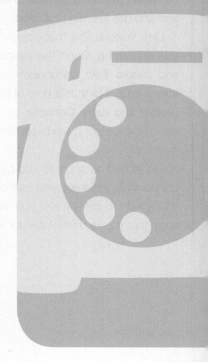

Perfect Birthday Gift

I'm waiting for my husband to ask me what I want for my birthday this year. I know just what I want. In the years before kids, he'd have gotten off easy with jewelry or clothes, dinner out, or a gift certificate to a day spa.

But after ten years and four kids, my idea of the perfect birthday gift has evolved. What I really want this year is four hours in my own bathroom, alone and uninterrupted. Just peace and quiet and porcelain.

I suppose this makes me a cheap date, but after ten years of doing whatever I've got to do in the bathroom in front of an audience, four hours of bathroom solitude sounds better than anything that can be put on a Master-Card.

My birthday fantasy looks like this: I'm loitering in the tub with my eyes closed. Around me there are no action figures, no stick-on alphabet letters, no naked Barbies. I want to let the water get as hot as I can stand it. I want to pick up a magazine, read an article from start to finish, and actually comprehend what I'm reading. I want to close the door and not have little notes slid underneath with my name on them, or see tiny fingers wiggling up at me.

Then I want to paint my nails — only mine, no one else's. I want to give myself a pedicure, a facial, and touch up my roots without once stopping to yell, "I'm in the bathroom. No, I can't come to you; you come to me!"

I don't care where my husband takes the kids. He'll think of something. I just want four hours to luxuriate in my own bathroom.

Hopefully while my husband is sitting in McDonald's play yard, staring at his watch, he'll remember his birthday is coming. Perhaps I'll tell him I'm toying with the idea of declaring the remote control off limits to anyone but Dad for that long, glorious afternoon. Consider the possibilities![6]

Just Say No

I was in the midst of running errands and had just settled into my car seat when I realized I had forgotten the bills I intended to mail. As I dashed inside, the phone rang.

"Hey, Mona," my friend said cheerfully. "I haven't seen you in ages. Want to get together today?"

"Uh, sure, what time?" I said, distracted by my to-do list. We set the time and place, and I hung up the phone.

Then, on my way back to the car, I did something that startled even me; I sat down on the big rock by my driveway and cried so hard, I couldn't catch my breath.

Later that night, after my three-year-old was tucked into bed, I pondered why my friend's phone call had brought me to tears. My emotional meltdown showed how stressed-out I was by life's demands, many of them self-induced. I needed to take better charge of my life.

The answer to my problem narrowed down to the simple word *no*. But the problem was that "yes" rolled off my tongue so easily, and "no" seemed cumbersome, even embarrassing. If someone needed snacks for the office, I'd bring them. If my child's playgroup was meeting, I organized not only the activity but the crafts. Add all this to working full-time plus, and it's no wonder I was exhausted.

Eventually I taped a neon sign saying "Just Say NO!" to my phone. Once I'd said no a few times, my lips began to form the word more confidently. It's still not easy to say no, but I'm gradually gaining more balance—and rest in my life.[7]

Take a Load Off

Drop everything.

That's easier said than done, right? You have places to go, people to see, things to do. You're constantly juggling school, work, family, friends, church. And you think that if you look away for even one second, everything could come crashing down.

Obviously, we all have plenty to do, and not all of it is going to affect the rest of our lives. We'd never get anything done, either, if we spent every minute asking ourselves, "Is this the absolutely best thing I could be doing right now?" But it's a question to think about now and then.

Do you have time to pray every day? Can you relax enough to enjoy a good book or a long walk outside? Is there room in your day for devotions and quiet time? In the midst of all you do, are there times you can just be with God?

Life was never meant to be a nonstop stress-fest. It's okay to slow down. In Matthew 11:28, Jesus says, "Come to me, all you who are weary and burdened, and I will give you rest."

So drop everything. Take a deep breath and rest for a while. You'll never lose the time you spend with Jesus.[8]

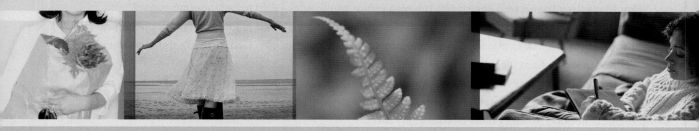

In the midst of all you do
are there times you can
just be with God?

A while back, I looked at my to-do list and noticed something terribly wrong. It wasn't so much what was on my list. The problem was what wasn't on my list: time for me.

Time for You

Before considering me selfish, stop a minute. As Christian women, we spend most of our time taking care of others—coworkers, friends, spouse, Sunday school students, children, roommates—and next to no time making sure we're rested and cared for.

I was on the brink of burnout, so I knew I had to make some changes. While I was sure a two-week vacation in a sleepy town in Italy would do the trick, I decided to settle for a few simpler and less budget-busting ways to pamper myself:

1. Celebrate relaxing traditions. My roommate and I love our annual Couch Potato Day, when we stay in our pajamas all day and watch three movies in a row. We usually schedule this during the bleak Chicago winter when being cozy indoors is a real treat. Another tradition I love is escaping to the local coffee shop over my lunch hour once a week to read my latest favorite book.

2. Nap. Some days I zoom home over my lunch hour, fit in a quick nap, and return to the office with fresh energy to tackle my in-box. Give me an hour, and I'm ready to take on the world.

3. Dream big, act small. Picture yourself five years from now. What do you hope you've accomplished, seen, or achieved from now until then? My big dream is to vacation in Italy. In the meantime I'm sending for tour brochures and reading a travel narrative about Italy. These little things make my big goal seem less distant.

At the heart of all these ideas is a simple principle: You're a priceless person created by God and you deserve to be treated as such. You're not being selfish; you're striving for balance. You can't meet everyone else's needs and do everything God has designed you for if you're running on empty.[9]

Truly my soul finds rest in God;
  my salvation comes from him.
Truly he is my rock and my salvation;
  he is my fortress, I will never be shaken.

Psalm 62:1–2

Come to me, all you who are weary and burdened, and I will give you rest. Take my yoke upon you and learn from me, for I am gentle and humble in heart, and you will find rest for your souls.

Matthew 11:28–29

He gives strength to the weary
and increases the power of the weak.
Even youths grow tired and weary,
and young men stumble and fall;
but those who hope in the LORD
will renew their strength.
They will soar on wings like eagles;
they will run and not grow weary,
they will walk and not be faint.

Isaiah 40:29–31

Chapter Four

Entertainment

Traveling Fun

Travel offers a shift in perspective, which is not about where you go or what you do as much as it is about being open to seeing what God is doing in the world around you.

For busy moms, travel may mean a girlfriend getaway to the beach or the mountains. Pack your prettiest pajamas and a pair of comfy shoes for exploring. Or perhaps you can join your husband on a business trip. Go sightseeing in a new city or take in a local art gallery while he's on the job.

Professional women can liven up their business trips by engaging in conversation on the plane instead of hiding behind a newspaper or book. Look for what makes your seatmate's eyes light up. In your free time, take a brisk walk along a lake, seeking an epiphany of the heart. Give God the gift of listening, and expect to hear his voice.

If you can't travel across the country or get a babysitter for a weekend, you can still seek adventure. If you live in the country, go into the city. Catch a trolley, serve people at a homeless shelter, or ride the glass elevator of a high-rise. If you live in the city, drive to the country for fresh produce, flowers, and a walk through muddy meadows. As the landscape around you changes, you'll notice changes in your point of view about your life circumstances.[1]

**He will yet fill your mouth with laughter
and your lips with shouts of joy.**

Job 8:21 NIV

Budget Travel Tips

When vacation season hits, do you look for ways to travel on the cheap? Here are ways to save some bucks as you hit the road or the friendly skies.

Stay home! Visit the local places you've always intended to go to "someday." A zoo or aquarium provides delight for any age, as do amusement parks, museums, and historical sites. Take in a semi-pro or professional sports game. Many outdoor theaters offer plays in the summer. Test your skills at boating or canoeing. I've found it best to plan a mini-trip each day of our at-home vacation. And I try my best not to clean or do tasks around the house. After all, it's vacation!
—Joyce Munn, Oklahoma

Try a house exchange. Trade your house or apartment with a friend or relative who lives in another state or country. This gives you a free place to stay, while you check out the area where your friend or relative lives. Ask for their advice on the best places to visit and eat. I've also seen people advertise for house exchang-es in newspapers and on websites. I know a retired couple that exchang-es time in their cabin so they can travel around the world at little cost.
—Alicia Alexander, Massachusetts

During the summer when college and university dorms are empty, many schools will rent you a room for the night. Usually you have to bring your own bedding and clean up after yourself, but it's an easy and inexpensive way to lodge.
—Jolie Goddard, via email

To save money on vacations, my family goes camping. On average, campground fees are about $25 per night, which is much lower than any hotel rate. We pack food to avoid res-taurant expenses; do no-cost activi-ties such as hiking or exploring U.S. national park presentations; do low-cost horse rides, rafting, or guided tours. What could be better than staying amid the beauty of God's cre-ation and sleeping under the stars?
—Holly Vergho, California

We go on vacation in June before the rates go up. Also, if we're go-ing to a beach, we look for a hotel that allows dogs. We found one that charges only five dollars extra for a dog. That's a lot cheaper than a ken-nel, and the kids loved being able to play with our dog on the beach.
—Tina Rogers, Pennsylvania

Get a hotel room that includes breakfast for you and the kids. Bring drinks and snacks for road trips to avoid pricey products at gas stations and tourist attractions. When possi-ble, we pack one of our meals, either lunch or dinner. When we eat out, we drink water instead of pop. This saves us money, plus it's healthier.[2]
—Tina Alt, Ohio

bad news fast

I think everyone should consider a media fast. No, I'm not talking about abstaining for a week from all television, videos, newspapers, and magazines.

What I am suggesting is a fast from all the bad news floating out there. Pick up the latest magazine from the grocery-store newsstand and cover copy shouts: "Will skin-eating bacteria endanger your family?" or "E.coli is out to get you!" or "What silent symptoms are YOU ignoring?" Grim financial outlooks, children killing children, white-collar crime—it seems that in today's world, nobody's honest, nobody's to be trusted, and nobody's sure we're going to survive into the next century.

That's why balance is so important. Yes, real life is sometimes hard, scary, and tragic. But it's also filled with hope, God's grace, and people who are loving, kind, and self-sacrificing. Life isn't all bad, dangerous, hazardous, and brimming with imminent disease, disaster, or death—even if a steady diet of the daily paper or evening news would have you think so.

Several months ago, I decided to cut back on the depressing stuff and concentrate on the upbeat. So instead of punching on CNN or Dateline, I sat down with my daughter, Emily, to watch I Love Lucy reruns. That became a nightly ritual. No matter how busy or tired I was, I made a point of sitting on the sofa with Em to laugh until tears rolled down our faces at Lucy's antics and Ricky's rolling eyes. After the show, the television went off. No ten o'clock news. And I never missed it.

The benefits were twofold. I spent precious time bonding with my daughter by cultivating a joint interest and I ended my day with vigorous laughter and happy thoughts instead of trauma, disaster, and mayhem. I found that when I limited what I exposed myself to for just a week, I felt more joyful and less fearful.[3]

VERTICLE HOLD

Media Choices

When my son Tony was young, it was simple to monitor his entertainment intake. Boundaries were easy; he could watch parent-approved videos such as Barney and a few Disney classics. But now that Tony is twelve, he wants to read comic books, watch action-packed movies, and listen to loud rap music.

As a parent, I worry about the negative messages my son receives from the media. Is he going to start cursing after hearing swear words in a song? Will he become violent because he reads Batman comic books? Will seeing an unmarried couple in bed together lead him toward premarital sex? How do I know which things to let him see, hear, or read, and which things to keep out of our home? And how will he respond if he's at a friend's house and someone pops in a video we'd deem inappropriate?

Tony's growing up and will soon have to make all his own media choices. Before he does, I want him to learn how to think critically when evaluating TV programs or movies.

Our family uses Philippians 4:8 NIV ("Whatever is true, whatever is noble, whatever is right, whatever is pure, whatever is lovely, whatever is admirable—if anything is excellent or praiseworthy—think about such things") to help us evaluate media choices. We list the qualities of this verse down the left side of a piece of paper—true, noble, right, pure, etc. Then we each pick a favorite movie, TV show, book, or music group to rate on the right-hand side.

After we've each rated our media choices, we share our thoughts and discuss them. My husband, Mike, might defend a secular group he enjoys because of the quality of its music. But he'll also admit the lyrics aren't such high quality. Tony may say that the show he rated presents many truths, but it also promotes actions that aren't admirable. We don't require that every form of entertainment meet all qualifications on this list, but we use the list as a starting point. At the end of our discussion, we decide together if our chosen program, movie, or book is something we should enjoy, limit, or cut out of our lives.[4]

How do I know which things to let him see,
hear, or read, and which things to
keep out of our home?

vacationing @ home

Let me be frank: in the past, our family vacations haven't been fun. First of all, traveling with three children, ages four to seven, is a challenge. Lengthy car rides result in squabbles — and not just among the children.

We eat too much fast food on our limited budget, and does anyone ever sleep well in a motel room?

As my husband and I considered destinations for last summer's vacation, we had this head-slapping realization: Why not stay home? We'd never taken advantage of the attractions in our own backyard because they were too expensive for everyday play. But if we funneled the money we'd budgeted for travel, hotel accommodations, and eating out into playing tourist in our own town, we'd finally get to enjoy those area attractions.

The surprise benefits of our homespun plans are the fond memories we now recall when we drive around town. Our children happily point to the museum we toured. And we all remember last-summer's ice cream cones when we pass our favorite ice-cream place in the dead of winter.

Vacationing at home is one of the smartest things we've done. The cost was minimal and the fun maximum. It also reminded us of the importance of playing with our children. Vacationing at home reminded us that recreation doesn't have to take work.

When you're planning your next family vacation, resist the urge to overbook. Spending time with your kids making special memories doesn't require lots of money or exotic destinations. Keep it simple. Have fun.[5]

While we agree that our ultra-cheap DVD dates bring us closer together as a couple, they also drag us into a gray area of morality and ethics. When it comes to entertainment, what's appropriate and what isn't?

watching what you watch

Is it okay to watch Russell Crow hacking away at arms and legs of enemies in Gladiator? Brad Pitt and Angelina Jolie sharing each other's bodies in marriage (*Mr. and Mrs. Smith*), while keeping secret their professional lives as skilled assassins? The trainer, father-figure Frankie Dunn (played by Clint Eastwood), pulling the plug on life support for the stricken female boxing champ in *Million Dollar Baby*?

All of those films, depending on whom you ask, have something positive to offer adult viewers. And every one of them, according to other observers, contains material inappropriate for anyone with a conscience.

"Every couple is different, but the one thing you can agree on is that we don't have that much time to spend together," says Michael Medved, ra-dio talk show host, former co-host of PBS's *Sneak Previews*, and book author. "If we decide to spend time watching something, let's limit it to something that might enrich our lives — maybe it makes us laugh, teaches us about history or just broadens our sense of what it means to be alive."

Quentin Schultze, professor at Calvin College and author of several books on Christians and the media, advises couples not to just wander through a video store and choose something they've never heard of, based on the box's description.

"My wife and I research films pretty well before we rent them," he says. "To just squander time on some meaningless two-hour video is worthless."

Once you're settled into your theater seat or living room couch, don't shut off your brain, either. Theater patrons used to throw rotten vegetables at the actors when the performance stunk. That might mean shutting off a video or walking out of a theater if a film turns out to be garbage. Escapism is one thing; exposing yourselves to something that assaults your values and sensibilities is quite another. Better to have wasted a little money than to burn a damaging image into your memory.

Bottom line: when you watch movies, engage your brain. Talk before you watch, and afterward. Decide your viewing standards as a couple. Recognize and avoid potentially destructive influences on your marriage and your spiritual life. And don't be afraid to stand up and throw vegetables once in a while.[6]

Girlfriend Time

Sure, we're busy. But we're never too busy for girlfriends, right? Here's how five women spend their time with girlfriends.

For sixteen years, my four sisters and I have enjoyed our annual girls' getaway weekend. Throughout the years our gatherings have included dinner theaters, pajama parties, board games, massages, horseback riding, and even playing on the swings at a park. No matter what we do together, we enjoy. Sometimes we laugh until our faces ache.

— Sue Augustine, New York

In the two years I've been driving a bus for physically challenged children, I've become friends with two other female bus drivers at our company. Our schedules allow us to meet for about forty-five minutes a day, which we used to spend gossiping and enjoying a smoke break at our company's headquarters. When guilt over those bad habits got the best of us, we decided to use this time to pray and read the Bible together. Now we look forward to our daily get-togethers. We even decided to stop smoking and to work out together at a local gym. God's making changes in our lives through our friendship with each other.

— Lisa Gallinger, New Hampshire

Each time my hubby has a computer game night at a friend's house, I invite a bunch of female friends over for a girlfriend night — doing things such as making greeting cards or an Olivia Newton-John movie marathon (she's popular here in Australia!). I invite a mix of friends from church, the moms' group to which I belong, and people I've known since college, so they can make new friendships while I'm deepening mine.

— Jen Wright, Australia

I'm part of a group of four women called the Heart-to-Heart Girls. For eight years we've gathered regularly to chat, pray, and eat out. Sometimes we do something fancier, such as enjoy a tea in a garden or attend a Christmas brunch. Through the years, we've watched God change our hearts and our marriages, and even free a couple women from addictions. Whatever we do, God is with us when we get together.[7]

— Katherine Behnke, Michigan

A friend loves at all times.

Philippians 17:17

Finally, brothers and sisters, whatever is true, whatever is noble, whatever is right, whatever is pure, whatever is lovely, whatever is admirable—if anything is excellent or praiseworthy—think about such things.

Philippians 4:8

everyday entertainment

You don't have to take a cruise or book a trip to Europe to have fun. You can make mini-vacations for yourself right at home just by trying something new. For example, last year I took a one-day class in which I learned how to make one of those expensive, handmade photo albums. It was a great break from my usual routine and launched a new hobby.

Restoring furniture is another kind of at-home entertainment. There's nothing like coming home from a brain-busting day at the office and sanding furniture. Really! I recently refinished a bookshelf and, after several tries, gave it an antiqued look. While my motives were mostly utilitarian—I needed a place to put my growing collection of cookbooks—the results were creative and freeing. Since we're made in the image of our Creator, we all possess creativity. What have you done with yours lately?

Strategically placing photos is another kind of fun. My roommate put a magazine ad with two men doing housework in the closet where we keep cleaning supplies. Every time I reach for the 409 cleaner or Windex, I laugh. Beat the drudgery of housework by putting photos of loved ones (or favorite comic strips) near your washer and dryer or the desk where you pay bills.

Have fun while driving, too. Next time you're alone in your car, turn off the radio and sing your favorite show tunes, nursery songs, hymns, or whatever makes you smile. It doesn't matter if you can't carry a tune or if the man in the next car looks at you funny—he's either sung a car solo himself sometime, or you've just given him a chuckle for the day.[8]

Chapter Five

Home & Hospitality

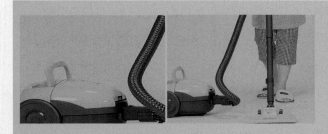

Cleaning House

After years of considering several theories about why I hated housekeeping, including my personal favorite that messy people aren't lazy but merely perfectionists gone awry, my husband spoke up. "Instead of reading about vacuuming," he said, straining not to sound peevish, "why don't you just vacuum?"

I won't go into my immediate response (something about his hands fitting around the vacuum handle as well as mine do). But I couldn't shake the nagging feeling he might be on to something.

I tried different strategies as I worked. I listened to books on tape to ease the monotony. I used a timer to keep me going for short bursts. I invited company over more often, finding humiliation avoidance to be an excellent motivator. I tried applying the verse that there's "a time to keep and a time to throw away" (Ecclesiastes 3:6).

Slowly, I began to notice a change. There was a kitchen table in our kitchen. Once it was cleared, we could even eat on it!

Slowly, I began to notice a change. There was a kitchen table in our kitchen. Once it was cleared, we could even eat on it!

As I kept cleaning, unearthing more discoveries by the month, a strange sense of peace began to emerge in our home. Perhaps tidying or putting stuff away wasn't so much bondage to chores. Perhaps it actually allowed me freedom to enjoy my home and family and to find a pencil with a point when I needed it.

No one ever will mistake my home for the National Institute of Perfect Order. Despite my best efforts, I'm not the cleaning fairy and never will be. But as I've gone down that painful path of change, seeking to learn from others, accepting my natural bend toward creativity yet working toward a more orderly existence, an amazing thing has happened.

I've become a good (okay, okay) homemaker. Seems there's no go-

ing back. As for my husband, who instigated all this, he's thrilled at the progress. In an effort to do his part, he has even discovered that his hands fit around the handle of a vacuum cleaner just fine.

And you ought to see that man with a squeegee.[1]

By wisdom a house is built,
    and through understanding it is established;
through knowledge its rooms are filled
    with rare and beautiful treasures.

Proverbs 24:3–4

a truly beautiful home

While it may seem silly or worldly to focus overmuch on decorating our homes, beauty does matter to our Creator, who is the author of it. Understanding that, I realized that while seeking beauty alone in our homes is hollow, there is nothing wrong with enhancing our dwelling places, making them the best they can be.

When I look at the beauty God created in nature, wondrously crafting the details of the world, I am overwhelmed with his love for me.

By making my home orderly and attractive, I communicate my love to those who live under my roof as well as those we invite to eat or stay with us. We can make others the priority when we are decorating our homes. We want our homes to be places that draw people in. We're not talking about spotlessness and perfection here; rather beauty, color, and light. We're talking anything that communicates love and care.

This is especially true for our husbands. We want to create an environment that will welcome them home to a place that's attractive, orderly, and clean. The end result is not creating a beautiful structure as much as an atmosphere in which people are blessed. It's not about the stuff. It's about using the stuff to make a place where people and relationships grow.[2]

"No one ever will mistake my home for the National Institute of Perfect Order"

Not long ago, I invited a neighbor and her little girl over to play. In my usual fashion, I made sure my floors were scrubbed, the furniture dusted, and every toy in its place.

Help from a Messy Neighbor

More than once during that visit, my neighbor remarked on how amazingly clean my house was, considering I had three young children. As she was leaving, she promised to have us over next time, but not until after she did some major cleaning at her house.

A few weeks later as we waved to one another from our yards, this same neighbor, suddenly inspired, motioned for me to come over. "I've been feeling guilty for not having you over yet, but my house is such a mess," she said. "So I figured if I let you come in today and see it at its worst, it won't stand in the way of a visit, anymore!" She proceeded to take me upstairs where she was in the midst of vacuuming, mopping, and changing beds. She even performed the "white glove test," displaying the failing results under my nose. Here was a woman who had no illusions about her own perfection.

I was humbled. What courage she demonstrated by inviting me to examine so closely what she considered to be lacking. I found myself in awe of her humility and eager for the freedom it

brought. My pride had been a millstone that I'd placed upon my own neck. It had almost killed a potential friendship. I wondered at the possibility of life without it.

The other day a friend called to say she'd be stopping by. My gut reaction said, "Quick—look good!" But this time my heart also reacted. As I surveyed the books and toys lying on the living room couch and the cracker crumbs littering the carpet, I realized that at this moment in life I was a mom with a messy house. Was I ready to admit that I couldn't keep up with everything today? How would my friend respond if I invited her into the place where I really live? Did I trust that she wouldn't reject me for being less than perfect?

I decided to leave everything the way it was. It wasn't easy; those few minutes while I was waiting for her to arrive were spent curbing a long-standing tendency to go into a cleaning panic. And I almost failed to resist the temptation to apologize for the mess. But I survived. We enjoyed our visit. And we're still friends.[3]

How Clean Is Clean?

While housework is necessary, it can be depressing because it's never done. You have just vacuumed your carpet, only to find your three-year-old has been trailing you with crackers, or worse, that your spouse has been trailing you with crackers. And when one person alone deals with cleanup, resentment can build quicker than scum on a shower wall. If you're feeling overwhelmed with housework, here are some steps on sharing the load:

1. Talk it out. All of us enter marriage with expectations on how our homes will run: the house is hers to take care of, or we'll each do 50 percent. But many times we don't clearly communicate those expectations to our spouse. Instead we assume the other will just get it. That is usually an incorrect—and unfair—assumption.

2. Define "clean." It's important to discuss what "clean" means for each of you. A common problem with housework is that we assume we're talking about the same thing when we're not. I value clean; my husband values tidy. I can walk by knitting projects strewn everywhere and not notice them, while he may never notice dust on a bookcase. Saying "Keep the living room clean" means different things to different people.

3. Delegate tasks. Once my husband and I understood each other's definition of "clean," it was easier for us to divvy up the housework. He makes sure things are picked up, and I concentrate on dusting and vacuuming.[4]

finding mentors

In the midst of some personal turmoil, my father moved three hours away to pastor a church, taking my mother—my closest confidante—with him.

"Whom will I talk to now?" I thought in a panic. "Who will offer me parenting advice and encourage me to hang in there?" We couldn't afford extended conversations by phone. And I didn't know the older women at church well enough to talk to them about my day-to-day concerns. I began praying about my need, but as the days passed, no one volunteered to mentor me. I realized I'd have to seek the godly counsel I needed.

Then one day on a Christian radio program, I heard Vonette Bright, author of *The Joy of Hospitality*, talk about hosting holiday teas and coffees.

I decided to go for it.

I started by placing an insert in the church bulletin inviting women at church to a Christmas tea. On a chilly December morning, fifteen women showed up at my home to hear about how to have a "fruit-filled Christmas." I chose that theme because we all tend to lack patience, joy, self-control, and other fruits of the Spirit in December, when we ought to have these godly virtues the most.

As we munched on sweet bread and sipped tea and wassail, we also read portions of the Christmas story from Luke 2, sang hymns, and discussed various topics, such as materialism, which I've struggled with.

One woman shared stories of having very few dishes to wash while raising seven children during the Great Depression. They only had turnips to eat twice a day for an entire winter. That inspired gratitude.

Because several of the women had lost loved ones, we bonded by praying about our losses, job changes, and other needs and burdens. Mature Christian women have an assurance that a lot of younger women like me don't have. They've been through more and know that God is always faithful.[5]

"one woman shared stories of
having very few dishes
to wash while raising seven children
during the great Depression"

the best part of entertaining

Jesus had a friend who knew all about juggling everything and who felt like if she looked away for one second, everything would come crashing down. It was poor, frazzled Martha.

Jesus had a friend who knew all about juggling everything and who felt like if she looked away for one second, everything would come crashing down. It was poor, frazzled Martha.

You can just imagine what was going on in her head as she tried to prepare Jesus' supper: "Bake the bread. Lay out the tablecloth. Arrange the fruit. You'd think Mary could come back here and help, wouldn't you? But no-o-o. Not her. She knows I'm in the kitchen, slaving away, and she's just sitting there, listening to Jesus. Who does she think she is, anyway?"

Martha was ticked. She stormed out of the kitchen and complained to Jesus, "Lord, don't you care that my sister has left me to do the work by myself? Tell her to help me!" (Luke 10:40).

Martha thought she had to be Super Hostess: cook, waitress, and maid, all in one. She couldn't see past the immediate, picky details of entertaining an honored guest. She was blinded by her own busyness.

Jesus responded, "Martha, Martha, you are worried and upset about many things, but few things are needed—or indeed only one. Mary has chosen what is better, and it will not be taken away from her" (Luke 10:41–42).

Martha stopped dead in her tracks. A bundle of napkins fell to the floor. She didn't notice. She had finally set her eyes on Jesus, and everything else faded into the background.

Martha had been missing out on the joy of fellowship with Jesus. That was the one thing she really needed. And it was the only thing that made everything else she did worthwhile.

Jesus didn't tell Martha that what she was doing was wrong. Cooking and serving and cleaning up aren't bad things, just like school, work, family, friends, and church aren't bad things. All of these things are very good, which is why it's so easy to let them dominate our day-planners.

Jesus simply told Martha that Mary's choice was better. Martha's cooking was fine, but it would only last until the food was all eaten. Mary's experience of listening to Jesus would affect her forever.[6]

> **But as for me and my household, we will serve the LORD.**
>
> Joshua 24:15

When it comes to entertaining others in your home, the most important thing is to shift your focus off yourself (the way you look, your house looks, or your meal turns out) and onto the folks who are coming to visit.

The Heart of Hospitality

It's not a mistake that the root of hospitality is hospital. The point is to open yourself up to other folks by letting them see the real you in your natural habitat so that they will open up to you. Every person, no matter how beautiful or perfect or successful they appear, has a unique set of special hurts or worries. Maybe all someone needs is for you to pay attention to them and to love them enough to invite them over for an impromptu burger off the grill.

"God created people for relationships," says marriage and family therapist Beverly Burch. "The only thing that was not good about Creation was that Adam was alone. He needed a partner. Because we are relational beings, isolation breeds depression. Opening your home opens the door to new relationships, or more supportive ones, both for you and those who come over."

As you focus on the needs and pleasure of your guests, you actually take the pressure off yourself because you realize hospitality isn't about showing off your cooking, cleaning, and decorating achievements. Your kind, intentional attention is more important to your friends than the fleeting pleasure of a spectacular dinner or phenomenal decorating.[7]

These commandments that I give you today are to be upon your hearts. Impress them on your children. Talk about them when you sit at home and when you walk along the road, when you lie down and when you get up. Tie them as symbols on your hands and bind them on your foreheads. Write them on the doorframes of your houses and on your gates.

Deuteronomy 6:6–9

The Lord's curse is on the house of the wicked,
but he blesses the home of the righteous.

Proverbs 3:33

Chapter Six

Safety

For in the day of trouble
　　he will keep me safe in his dwelling;
he will hide me in the shelter of his tabernacle
　　and set me high upon a rock.

Psalm 27:5

Confidence Builders

In a world of terrorism, crime, and natural disasters, much of the security we once took for granted has been shattered. When you feel especially shaky about safety in troubled times, turn to God and ask for guidance. Some things to keep in mind:

1. Keep believing. Jesus said, "In this world you will have trouble. But take heart! I have overcome the world" (John 16:33).

2. Teach your children right from wrong. Make clear that evil does exist, but that it won't go unpunished.

3. Show empathy. It's our duty to heal those who hurt, comfort those who are lost, restore those who've gone astray, love those who are embittered. As you practice faith through love, people will find hope.

4. Take comfort in God's Word. Study it now more than ever. Psalm 119:105 reminds us that the Bible is a lamp to our feet and a light for our path.

5. Look for God in everything. See God's hand in the spiritual hunger we see ignited in our nation.

6. Let your light shine. Without becoming obnoxious or pious, offer hope to nonbelievers. Speak tenderly to them about God's mercy, faithfulness, and plan for us.

7. Give thanks. God's promises stand firm even in the midst of pain. As 2 Chronicles 7:14 tells us: "If my people, who are called by my name, will humble themselves and pray and seek my face and turn from their wicked ways, then I will hear from heaven, and I will forgive their sin and will heal their land." God always keeps his promises.[1]

why I survived

One hundred twenty-five Pentagon employees died September 11, 2001, and my division lost half its staff to death or injury. I could have been among that number, but God chose to lead me safely away from danger.

Many times I've asked myself since: "Why did he save me and not others?" Nearly three years have passed, and I still don't have answers.

In the weeks following the incident, I struggled with the sorrow of losing so many co-workers, but at the same time I recognized that death is an inescapable part of life. Where, when, and how we leave this earth is God's decision. The Lord is completely just in his actions, and I trust in his unfailing love. I believe his hand was upon the survivors, leading them to safety. And for those whose time had come, I'm certain he was there to comfort them. My faith in Christ helped me to deal with the tragedy and gave me strength to move forward.

Because I survived, I'm certain God still has work for me to do. And knowing he saved me for a purpose only increases my determination to do all I can for him while I live. Life is a gift, one I'll use to bring him glory.

Thankfully, days such as 9/11 are rare, but the lessons we learn from them remain. God never promised that when we promised to serve him, our lives would be free from trouble, pain, or sorrow. But he did promise never to leave us or forsake us (Hebrews 13:5). Those who put their trust in him have this hope: No matter what happens, God is always with us.[2]

"Because I survived, I'm certain God still has work for me to do."

Surviving Identity Theft

My wallet was stolen while I was having chemotherapy in a Chicago hospital. Before the nightmare ended, the thieves had altered my driver's license, written checks totaling more than $6,000, and racked up dozens of charges on various credit cards. **Through that experience, I've learned some lessons about preventing victimization through ID theft** >>>

1. Travel light. A friend who also had her purse stolen in the city says she now wears a backpack and tucks one credit card and a little cash in an inside pocket or in her shoe. Likewise, I've learned to leave my checkbook and most credit cards at home when I'm traveling. I've also separated my checkbook from a small wallet so the person who might get one doesn't get all.

2. Be organized. Someone at work suggested periodically writing down all the contents in your wallet. You might take that a step further. Write down all the credit-card contact numbers so that if your cards are stolen, you can quickly report the theft and cancel the cards.

3. Don't take the blame. The cashier who rejects my check because there's a hold on my account doesn't mean to be rude; she's just doing her job. On the other hand, I don't have to feel compelled to explain myself. I can fight for my reputation in other ways than blabbing the details of the theft to a perfect stranger.

4. Don't give up. It's been six months since the theft, and I've grown weary of cleaning up after it. Yet I can't quit until the last registered letter is answered and the final check accounted for. My financial reputation depends on it.

5. Use your experience to help others. Several months after the theft, a coworker gave her friend Susie my number. Susie's purse had been stolen while she was eating dinner at a Chicago restaurant. After listening to her story and walking her through the procedures for damage control, I heard something that cut to the heart. "Tell me, Phyllis, are you ever afraid that these people might come after you? They have all your personal information, including where you live."

I'd thought about that after my wallet was stolen. I prayed about it. And I came to realize that the thieves didn't want me—just my money.

When I told Susie that, she started crying. "You'll be fine," I reassured her. "God will take care of you."

Thieves can get your money, your credit cards, and your checkbook. They can steal your financial identity, but they can't steal you. That belongs to Jesus. And that's 100 percent secure from any identity theft.[3]

Harassment At Work

Sexual harassment is unwanted, repeated sexual attention at work. It can take many forms: inappropriate gifts; unwelcome hugging or touching; telling intimate details of one's sexual life; sexual jokes, innuendos or stories; excessive compliments, especially about appearance; graphic descriptions of sexual material such as pornography; repeated phone calls or pressure for dates; rude noises such as lip-smacking, whistling, or hooting; and stalking.

Sexual harassment is illegal. So if you think you're being victimized by it, take action. Some steps you can take to stop it:

1. Ask questions. Do some research. Call the U.S. Equal Employment Opportunities Commission (800-669-4000) and ask for the office nearest you. Also obtain counseling, information, and even free legal advice through 9 to 5, a nonprofit organization helping working women with problems on the job (800-522-0925).

2. Say no. Clearly communicate your disapproval of any sexually inappropriate behavior. Don't smile or apologize; either sends a confusing signal.

3. Name the behavior. Whatever the harasser is doing—telling a dirty joke, touching you, whistling—repeating what's being done out loud often stops the behavior immediately.

4. Put it in writing. If speaking to the person is too uncomfortable, write a letter identifying the objectionable behavior. State your feelings about it and that you expect it to stop. Keep a dated copy of your letter.

5. Enlist others. If attempts to deal directly with your harasser fail, get others involved. Matthew 18:15-17 offers an outline for confrontation: "Go and point out the fault, just between the two of you." If that doesn't work, "take one or two others along" as witnesses: likeminded coworkers, the harasser's supervisor, even your pastor. Most companies have a policy for dealing with sexual harassment.

6. Keep records. Matthew 18:17 offers a final guideline: Consider going public. To prepare, log all incidents involving your harasser. Be specific about words and actions used, the date, time, and place, and who may have witnessed the incident. Photocopy any offensive materials such as cartoons or memos. Evidence is important if you decide to file a complaint.

7. Obtain copies of your work records. Keep them at home. Whenever you have a performance review, be sure to get a copy of it to add to your home file.

8. Consider legal options. You may file a formal complaint with the Fair Employment Practice Agency or the Equal Employment Opportunity Commission. File within 180 days after the incident. Experts recommend retaining an attorney when you first decide to make your complaint. Even if you've not confronted your harasser, you may be eligible for compensation for lost wages and benefits, attorney fees, injunctive relief (changes in workplace policy), or punitive damages.[4]

Ignited by arsonists in the morning, the blaze in Southern California had exploded. By early afternoon most of the town had evacuated.

God's Hand in the Fire

We were among the last to leave our house in the mountains. I glanced one last time at Tony, my husband of sixteen years, wondering if this was our final moment together. Our son, Joshua, and I would seek safety in the desert below, while Tony, a firefighter, would stay behind. "I can handle returning to no home," I thought, gazing skyward. "But, Lord, please protect my husband."

For four sleepless nights, we moved constantly, not knowing if we would ever return to our home. Finally, an unexpected storm hit, dropping steady rain and eventually snow on the burn area.

When Tony finally called, my heart leapt with joy. He was alive and well. Our home, too, was still standing.

After we reunited, Tony told us how he initially felt abandoned by God as he watched the fire devour thirty-five homes, then rush through Devil's Canyon. The turning point came on Wednesday. Tony's crew didn't have enough water or manpower to stop the fire, but mysteriously the flames started to sputter out. It was as though a supernatural force was with them. Tony's mind flashed to Isaiah 43:2: "When you walk through the fire, you will not be burned."

After the fire was under control, Tony looked at a fire map in the command center. Crestline was in the middle with red all around it. Tony couldn't shake the image of what looked like a hand resting over our town.

"This is what God did," Tony told me after we were reunited.

I feared that fire would take everything from us. But God only allowed it to take the things my husband and I no longer needed: doubt and fear. Like the refiner who hovers over his creation to ensure it's purified, not destroyed by fire, God was and is always near us.[5]

Safety in the Dark

While it's good to be wary of protecting yourself at all times and in various surroundings, it's especially important to be aware of taking precautions when it's dark outside. Here are a few stay-safe tips from the American Women's Self-Defense Association:

1. Park in well-lit areas or close to the front door of wherever you're going.
2. Keep your hands free to be able to fight off a potential attacker. Strap your purse around your head or inside your coat.
3. Walk with confidence so you don't look like an easy target.
4. Get some training in self-defense at your local community college or parks and recreation department.
5. Trust your instincts. If you feel someone is following you, immediately go to a crowded or well-lit area.[6]

peace in waiting

Shortly before Darren Davis left for Operation Iraqi Freedom, his family had a family picture taken. "It was one of those things you do, just in case," says Darren's wife, Carla.

Carla is very concerned about her husband's safety. "I'm not normally a worrier, but I've had a few sleepless nights," says the thirty-seven-year-old mother of two young children. "I've had some dark times when I've wondered why Darren is where he is and why our children have to go through months without their daddy.

"It's been a difficult time, but through it all, I've felt God at my side. He always comes through at exactly the moment I need him. I can't imagine facing these uncertain times without God. He sustains me when my strength is gone and my worries surface."

Carla clings to favorite Scriptures in these difficult days, such as Psalm 55:16–18:

"I call to God,
    and the LORD saves me.
Evening, morning and noon
    I cry out in distress,
    and he hears my voice.
He rescues me unharmed
    from the battle waged against me."

One side effect of the war, says Carla, is that it brings opportunities to share her faith.

"Many people have asked me how I'm able to deal with what's going on," she says. "I tell them my faith in God and his love for me sustains me. They're usually open to hear what I have to say."[7]

Protection from Abuse

According to Detective Sgt. Don Stewart, a retired police officer who handled domestic violence cases for twenty-five years, one of every four Christian women experiences at least one episode of physical abuse within marriage.

Battering is the single largest cause of injury to women. Women have more injuries due to physical abuse from their husbands than from auto accidents, muggings, and rapes combined. According to The American College of Obstetricians and Gynecologists, three to four million women are beaten in their homes every year. About two thousand women are beaten to death, says the U.S. Department of Justice. So how can a woman tell if a man is a potential batterer? "Look out for jealousy, hypersensitivity toward even the most constructive criticism,

and the tendency to pressure you into a quick engagement, marriage, or live-in relationship," Stewart says. "Other indications include any use of physical force against you or an unusually harsh attitude toward children or animals. And any history of past battering should be of major concern."

What if you're in a relationship you fear could become physically abusive?

Stewart advises, "When a husband starts saying things such as, 'If you ever left me, I'd kill myself,' or 'If you don't do exactly as I tell you, I'm going to beat the daylights out of you,' those are clues that verbal abuse may be escalating to physical abuse."

Another sign is when a husband starts damaging items that his wife values. "A batterer never will demolish his prized

possessions, but he often will shatter a piece of pottery or a family heirloom," Stewart says. "If his comments intensify to the point that he says something such as, 'If you ever leave me, I'm going to kill you and the kids,' or 'I'm going to burn the house down,' he's crossed a critical psychological barrier. It's not long before he's going to act on his words."

When a woman hears words like that, she should immediately make arrangements to find protection elsewhere. "You may have to leave only until you and your husband can get some counseling or until he's arrested and has gone through a treatment program," Stewart says, "but you need to remove yourself from the dangerous situation."[8]

"Look out for jealousy and hypersensitivity toward even the most constructive criticism."

internet dating

I admit it; I'm one of those kooky people who started dating a stranger
I met online, then ended up marrying him.

I still feel embarrassed when I tell our story. That's because it wasn't just the Internet that brought my husband, Alexei, and me together, but it was the personal ad I placed there. I used to swear I'd never do such a thing; I thought it was silly and hinted at desperation. Plus I was certain a personal ad was no way to meet a healthy individual and develop a lasting relationship. But one evening, God's nudging changed all that.

Meeting people online can be dangerous, so you really need to use your head when you try this arena. For example, I didn't send my photograph to the men who asked for it upfront because I wanted some indication first that the person was looking for a God-centered, committed relationship, not just for a shallow fling.

I also didn't give out any personal information at first. It's vitally important you don't tell anyone where you live (not even the city), your last name, your address, or your phone number. Only after I got more comfortable with someone did I give out my phone number (since you can only tell so much about a person from his emails).

Also keep in mind that anyone you meet online has all the control about the information you learn about him. He easily can send you a photograph of someone else and try to pass it off as himself and can make up details about his life. Many of the ways we get to know people in person don't apply to online relationships. You can't hear someone's tone of voice when you're emailing and you can't read his body language when you're instant-messaging him or talking on the phone. Always be aware that there are people on the Internet whose sole intent is to deceive you.

When and if you do agree to meet someone in person, be sure to meet in a public place, the first time and several times after that. Arrange to meet somewhere so you can drive yourself home. Also, let the man come your way, especially if you live a long distance away from each other. Meeting him on your turf will make you feel more comfortable and also will test how great his interest is in you.

Be cautious when you meet and communicate with someone online. If a guy pressures you to move forward with your relationship faster than you're comfortable, don't give in. If he's truly seeking a serious relationship and respects you, he'll wait till you're ready.[9]

Protecting Kids Online

Kids who get into danger online are almost always the ones whose parents have not taken an active role in their online experience. The good news is that you as a parent can do much to keep your kids safe by making them cyber-smart. Cover these basics with your kids:

1. Discuss safety in cyberspace. Many children are drawn to the web for its potential to build relationships, but they know little or nothing about its potential dangers. You might wish to use the Internet with your kids or direct them toward positive websites to get them started.

2. Use monitored chat rooms. If you allow your children to participate in online chats, insist that they only participate in chat rooms monitored by approved adults trained to keep conversations appropriate. Remember that not all people you meet online are who they say they are.

3. Keep the computer in view. Children who use the Internet with parents in view are less likely to engage in dangerous conversations.

4. Keep personal information private. Tell your kids not to disclose any personal information, such as last name, city, gender, age, or school name during an online chat. Also, don't allow them to send their picture, passwords, or any credit card information over the Internet without getting your permission.

5. Prohibit in-person meetings. Don't allow your kids to personally meet anyone they meet online.

6. Report suspicious incidents. If your children feel they are being stalked online, immediately contact law enforcement officials and your Internet service provider. You can call the FBI's Cyber Tipline (800-843-5678) if you suspect that your child is involved in a potentially dangerous situation.

7. Limit accessibility. Software can help you control your children's access to potentially hazardous areas in cyberspace. These web filters block objectionable websites, chat rooms, and other areas that are inappropriate for your children.

8. Use special Internet providers. A number of Internet Service Providers (ISPs), some of them Christian companies, block objectionable websites before they reach your computer without requiring separate filtering software. You don't need a separate web filter once you have one of these filtered ISPs.[10]

security for kids

Christians know that true security doesn't lie in metal detectors, video surveillance, community resources, or law enforcement.

It comes with having a personal relationship with an almighty, sovereign God. Nothing surprises him. He doesn't wake up one morning and wring his hands, wondering, "Oh, my. What shall I do?"

With that in mind, help your child discover the following:

1. God is our refuge. "Those who fear the LORD have a secure fortress, and for their children it will be a refuge," says Proverbs 14:26. Tell your child, "Even if I'm not with you, God is. When you're afraid, you can talk to him."

2. God is our protector. Proverbs 2:8 says that God "guards the course of the just and protects the way of his faithful ones." Make a collage from magazine clippings and labels from products that promise to protect us. Write this verse from Proverbs in bold letters across the collage.

3. God is our powerful shepherd. Isaiah 40:10–11 tells us: "See, the Sovereign LORD comes with power, and his arm rules for him. See, his reward is with him, and his recompense ac-

companies him. He tends his flock like a shepherd: He gathers the lambs in his arms and carries them close to his heart; he gently leads those that have young." This is a compelling picture of our tough and tender leader.

Ask your child to describe some things that are both tough and tender. Then read the verses from Isaiah and describe how a shepherd needs to be tough enough to take on mountain lions but tender enough to care for a lamb. When we build these powerful concepts into the lives of our kids, we are building emotional and spiritual fences of protection and security around their lives. These boundaries don't lead to bondage; they lead to freedom. As the psalmist wrote: "I run in the path of your commands, for you have set my heart free" (Psalm 119:32).[11]

Love on a Leash

After paying for our groceries, I looked back at my son to see how he liked the snack I had bought him, but he was gone. I glanced around frantically and asked his sister, "Where's Knox?" She shrugged.

"He's out in the parking lot," two employees casually informed at the door.

I dashed outside to find my toddler running with his hand in the air, proudly displaying his treat. Seeing that he was headed for traffic and running much faster than I could, I screamed his name. That slowed him enough for me to catch the tag on his shirt. I grabbed it and held on.

Breathless, I walked back into the store with Knox in tow. I gathered my things and looked around at the small gathering of bystanders judging my mothering skills.

In the car, I couldn't speak. I couldn't move. I felt nauseated. I cried uncontrollably. Though my son sat safely in his car seat, I couldn't let it go.

I struggled emotionally for days over this incident. I talked with God over and over, thanking him, praising him, and asking for forgiveness. I couldn't let it go; I worried that Knox might wander off again. Then I had an epiphany: Buy a leash.

The day that I finally invited Jesus into my life, a leash of sorts was attached to me. To protect me, God sent the Holy Spirit to guide me and connect me to him. He holds on to me always, only a short length away. Likewise a leash might help keep my toddler safe. So, the next day I went into a different store, where I whispered to the clerk, "Do you carry leashes for children?" She smiled politely and motioned for me to follow her to the safety section, where there were only three leashes for children left.

I took Knox with me to the drugstore that day on a leash. As we walked down the aisle, a young woman looked at me with disdain. I looked at my son, who held up a box of cookies. "Put them back, please," I said. Knox smiled and tugged me to our next stop.

Judge me, if you must. I thank God for the leash.[12]

a grip on fear

More than three hundred times in the Bible, God tells us not to fear. One way to stop being anxious about your child's safety is to think about God's promises. Take every fearful thought captive and say, "Yes, there's potential for violence, but I choose to stress the good things of God."

That doesn't mean you're in denial, rather, that you're choosing to trust God with your child, no matter what.

Philippians 4:6 tells us not to be anxious about anything, but to be thankful. Many people wonder if that means they're supposed to thank God for the violence. Of course not. You're supposed to thank God that his promises are real and that you can trust him with your child.

What happens when you do that is that you move from asking God to give you peace, to interceding for the kids whose hearts are so troubled they want to commit violent acts. We can work in the cultural media, we can work at getting prayer back in the schools, we can work at getting family problems corrected, or we can work at identifying depressed kids. But the only real solution to violence is changing the hearts of kids through the power of Christ.[13]

The name of the LORD is a fortified tower;
the righteous run to it and are safe.
Proverbs 18:10

Discretion will protect you,
and understanding will guard you.
Proverbs 2:11

Chapter Seven

Leaving a Legacy

Godly Womanhood

My daughter ultimately will follow someone's model of womanhood. I pray I'm the one she emulates. I want what I model to point clearly to Jesus Christ. For example, as I learn to submit or to forgive others, I set a godly example for Corinne. Submission is hard for me — I like to have the last word, and I share my opinions freely — so I work on that daily. As my daughter sees my continuing struggle, she'll be a little farther along in her own life of submission.

The lifestyle choices we make dramatically affect our daughters. For example, a recent study in *Pediatrics* magazine reported that 88 percent of the daughters of teen mothers also become teen mothers. These same daughters of teen mothers are 3.6 times more likely to receive public financial support than the daughters of older mothers. The choices we make — biblical or not — affect our daughters in ways we can't foresee.

If you're like me, you pray your daughter will become a woman God can use and be proud of. While prayer avails much, we can give our daughters a head start on womanhood by the way we live our lives. Years from now, when my daughter, Corinne, sees me staring back at her from the mirror, I hope she'll know I tried to do the job God called me to do when he gave me a daughter.[1]

my proverbial grandma

My grandma was a Proverbs 31 woman. She was worth far more than rubies (v.10). As a farmer's wife, she worked with her hands from sunup to sundown, providing food for her family (v.15).

I'll always remember her flourishing garden of tall corn and leafy vines of cucumbers, zucchini, squash, and watermelon. I loved watching her dig up potatoes, beets, turnips, radishes, and carrots with her rusty metal spade. She washed and canned the vegetables, storing jars of them in the cool, dark root cellar.

Before sunrise she milked the cows. As the sun peeked over the horizon, she was shucking corn for the chickens and gathering eggs for baking. Grandma cooked enough food so no one left the table hungry.

She'd leave the "nibble leftovers" on the table for passersby, and the cookie jar was never empty. The bread of idleness was not for her (v. 27).

At night Grandma relaxed by making quilts or crocheting afghans, scarves, and vests of wool and cotton for her family (v. 13).

Grandma worked hard six days a week, but when Sunday came her routine changed. Every Sunday Grandma went to Sunday school and church. After services Grandpa, Grandma, Mom, and I squeezed into the front seat of Grandpa's navy blue 1961 Ford pickup to visit relatives. When an evangelist came to town, Grandma took my cousin and me to revival meetings.

Although it's hard to be a Proverbs 31 woman today, I try to model my dear grandma who taught Proverbs to me by example.[2]

mentors all

When Titus 2 talks about older women teaching younger women, I thought it meant older women, like ninety or so. But God totally busted me on that thinking. He challenged me to realize that as long as there's someone on this planet younger than I am, she's mine to teach. That's why I'm using "God Chicks" events to invest in young women and to challenge them to invest in girls younger than they are.

That said, I realize I couldn't do these conferences if I didn't have an amazing company of older women who not only are getting inspired themselves, but are also here to cheer on younger women.

When the women at our events understand they have a responsibility to the next generation, that motivates them to live life well. Knowing others are watching keeps us accountable.

About eighteen months into our marriage, my husband, Philip, and I weren't connecting. I was expecting him to be someone he wasn't instead of accepting him the way he was. He wasn't making me happy, and I thought that was his job. I thought I'd missed God's leading and had married the wrong guy. I packed my bags and prepared to leave.

Two things made me stay. First, I realized I loved God and was unwilling to disobey his commands about marriage and divorce. And second, an older woman came into my life and mentored me. She was open about lessons she had learned in her marriage and walked with me through this tough time.

Philip and I have now celebrated our twenty-year anniversary. I know part of what got us here was that older woman who invested in me. And I knew that I, in turn, am expected to play that role in someone else's life.[3]

The choices we make —biblical or not— affect our daughters in ways we can't forsee

Legacy of a Single Woman

I think we all want to make a lasting difference with our lives. But there are times when we singles can think our lives don't amount to much and that if we never marry, our existence on this earth will just be a blip on the screen of history.

Producing and nurturing a loving Christian family is a great thing to show for one's time on this earth. But I also think of the customers in my single friend Kate's shop, whose day she brightens with her warm smile and Christlike kindness. I think of the refugees and immigrants in my ESL (English as a Second Language) class, and the people who read the book I wrote for singles. Hopefully God is blessing them through me.

I also think of the young single woman I saw at my favorite coffee shop the other night, leading her new-believer friend in a Bible study. And I think of the many people my former roommate touched during the two years she taught English and built strategic friendships with unbelievers in Mongolia.

With all these unmarried folks and so many more in mind, I think about the freedom we have as singles to leave legacies to children, coworkers, homeless people, unbelievers, and a host of others. Whether my singleness is temporary or lifelong, I want to be able to look back someday and say, "That's what God used to help me make a lasting impact."

Thinking this way makes me consider more strategically how I live, realizing that lasting meaning and impact can start now, not in some far-off someday when and if a husband and kids enter the picture. I am asking God to show me the lasting work he wants to do in and through my singleness. I'm excited to see where he leads.[4]

mothers and grandmothers

Mothers and grandmothers can have a powerful spiritual impact on their families. Through these godly women, many of us see Jesus for the first time. Before we can even speak, we breathe in the heavenly aroma of Christ. And as we watch our mothers and grandmothers, we see in them the light that has come into the world.

In 2 Timothy 1:5 Paul says to Timothy, "I am reminded of your sincere faith, which first lived in your grandmother Lois and in your mother Eunice and, I am persuaded, now lives in you also." Notice that Paul doesn't talk about Timothy's father or grandfather. Rather, he gives the credit for Timothy's faith to two godly women, Lois and Eunice.

Perhaps the men in Timothy's life weren't followers of Jesus. Some commentators think Acts 16:1, which describes Timothy's father as a Greek, suggests that.

Regardless, from this godly woman, Lois, came a legacy of faith that helped bring at least two generations into the family of God. Lois, a Jew, accepted Jesus as her Savior, possibly only a decade or two after Jesus' death and resurrection. Coping with any objections her husband may have had, she brought up her daughter, Eunice, in the Christian faith. Eunice did the same with her son, Timothy.

The effect of Lois and Eunice's godly legacy is apparent to readers of the New Testament. Thanks to their witness, Timothy became a powerful force in the early church, bringing the gospel to hundreds, even thousands of people.

If your mother or grandmother has passed on a legacy of faith to you, thank her. No one can inherit faith, of course, but godly mothers and grandmothers can at least make sure that Jesus is never a stranger to their children and grandchildren.[5]

scrapbook of faith

When four of my friends became Creative Memories consultants, I began attending scrapbook parties. In those parties, my friends frequently mentioned that photos are one of the most powerful ways to remember people and events.

I had to agree. I had boxes filled with snapshots of my friends from every concert, play, picnic, or party we'd attended. But what became apparent to me after I bought bundles of colorful pens and cute paper was that our nights of fun were a part of our friendships, but not the best part. What I wanted to remember was the way my friend Tracy trusted God to provide for her when she lost her job. I needed a place to record the time Christy and I prayed in the church parking lot for an hour after a long night of ministry. I wanted to record what God was doing in each of our lives. Wasn't that the most exciting part, anyway?

So I began to chronicle our spiritual highs and lows alongside our beaming pictures. I included the verses we'd memorized or the prayers we'd said for each other, the encouraging cards I'd received or short stories that demonstrated the characteristics I most admired in each friend.

These photo journals became a record of how God has grown my loved ones and me. Just flipping through the pages, I can see so many reminders of God's goodness. In the face of such living proof, I'm always lifted up.

A Family of Faith Photo Journal can be a great way to teach your kids to remember God's work in their lives. Making one can be as simple as taking pictures at the start of each school semester and including a blank page to record the triumphs and challenges God brings your kids through. Or, you could build your album around important spiritual events in your family's life, such as each member's spiritual birthday.[6]

sandwiches of love

At three years old, my son made the worst sandwiches in the world. The bologna would hang off the bread, the cheese ended up in a ball, and the lettuce, well, that was typically picked off the floor and thrown away. Never mind that it would take a full five minutes to get a sandwich that was presentable; eventually it would get done. Only forty-nine to go!

I say these words with pride because those fifty sandwiches would eventually end up at our local homeless shelter. A side of chips, cookies, and an apple rounded out a meal that was welcomed by the shelter's clients.

My sons and I have been volunteering in various capacities for most of their lives. Sometimes we just help gather items for the Goodwill truck, but other times we bring food to our church or the local shelter. Sometimes that means making sack lunches for fifty people.

As a Christian, I have a little voice inside me nudging me to teach my son the value of helping those who are economically "least among us." As Jesus tells us in Matthew 25:40, "Truly I tell you, whatever you did for one of the least of these brothers and sisters of mine you did for me."[7] I welcome that little voice and pass its wisdom on to my sons.

maegan's legacy

Maegan had AIDS. She didn't know how sick she was, though she often asked why she had to take so much medicine and go to the doctor so often. I explained she had a disease and the doctors were trying to find the right medicine.

Once we drove by a church where a funeral was taking place. Maegan, who had lost her hearing, pointed at the hearse and signed, "Die ... what happened?" I answered that sometimes people are very sick and the doctors can't find the right medicine. She grinned at me and signed, "Momma, Jesus has the right medicine in heaven, doesn't he?" I blinked back tears and nodded yes.

Maegan began to talk about heaven constantly and draw pictures of the mansion that awaited her. She labeled the rooms, including the one that would be hers.

Jeff and I shook our heads in disbelief, because much of what she was saying didn't come from me, and up to that point I'd been her only teacher.

When Maegan asked to be baptized, I asked, "Do you know what baptism means?" She rolled her eyes and signed, "It means you believe in Jesus, and you know I believe!" My husband, Jeff, also made the decision to accept Christ. He and Maegan were baptized together.

Some people didn't understand Maegan's preoccupation with heaven. "She should be fighting to live,

Only be careful, and watch yourselves closely so that you do not forget
the things your eyes have seen or let them slip from your heart as long
as you live. Teach them to your children and to their children after them.

Deuteronomy 4:9 NIV

not talking about dying," her grandmother told me one
night. I wondered if she was right. But when I went to
Maegan's room for our bedtime story, she picked up her
Bible storybook and signed, "I want this story tonight."

The story was about mothers who brought their children to Jesus but were turned away by the disciples. Jesus scolded the disciples for sending the children away.
Chills ran up my spine as I read, "Let the little children
come to me, and do not hinder them, for the kingdom of
heaven belongs to such as these" (Matthew 19:14 NIV).
I could no longer dodge Maegan's questions, such as,

"Who will sign for me when I get to heaven?" and "What
happens to your body when you die?"

I had prepared Maegan for her first day of school and
her first dentist appointment. Now I would prepare her
for her journey home.[8]

ouch.

What you heard from me, keep as the pattern of sound teaching, with faith and love in Christ Jesus. Guard the good deposit that was entrusted to you—guard it with the help of the Holy Spirit who lives in us.

2 Timothy 1:13–14

A Pickle with Sunburn

When some parents think of spiritually training their children, they immediately think of family Bible studies or devotions. Those are valid tools, but to be honest, those things don't work with my kids. I've got three young boys and getting them to sit down together and work through a nice, quiet devotional is a real mind-stretcher.

So, my wife and I have learned to incorporate teaching moments into our routines. Meals, times spent in the car, and bedtime all offer potential for impromptu lessons. For example, the other day I started our dinner with a question: "What's green, bumpy, and red all over?" The answer: A pickle with sunburn.

The boys loved the joke. Everyone then had to think of a different kind of pickle. I said that one kind of pickle is a baseball pickle where you get stuck in the middle of two bases. Then I asked, "Who are some people in the Bible who got themselves into pickles? Was it their fault?"

The boys brought up Jonah and Moses. After reviewing those stories, each of us had to describe a personal pickle. We asked, "Was it your fault or not?" We ended with a short Bible verse. The whole thing took less than ten minutes.

These Mealtime Moments are a great way to steer discussion toward something spiritual. Most families eat a few meals together each week, so Mealtime Moments are easy to incorporate into your regular routine.

We did another kind of Moment in the car, where we gave the kids the map to help us get to McDonald's. I told my eight-year-old, "You tell me where to go." He said, "You turn right at this street."

I said, "Aah, I know where I'm going. I don't need the map." I took a left.

Boy, did my son get upset. He really wanted to go to McDonald's, and I kept ignoring his directions. After several wrong turns, we ended up in a dead-end alley. My son yelled, "Dad, you are supposed to follow the directions!"

We then talked about how the Bible gives us directions for our lives. It took us five minutes out of our way, but the lesson had a significant impact on my son. It was a great contribution to our spiritual heritage.[9]

The Truth About Money

Money problems are in our head.

So says popular author and financial adviser Suze Orman. "The road to financial freedom begins not in a bank or even in a financial planner's office," she writes in *The Nine Steps to Financial Freedom*. "It begins with our thoughts. And those thoughts, more often than not, stem from our seemingly forgotten past with money."

Orman's words prompted me to explore my own thoughts about money. It dawned on me that perhaps there was part of me that didn't want to know about money matters and who wanted someone else (a husband?) to take care of the finances — and, by extension, to care for me.

If we want to move beyond our thoughts and fears about money, we need to replace them with God's truth about our finances. I had previously read, even studied, many Bible passages on wealth, but now I found dozens more passages, from straightforward admonitions — "Let no debt remain outstanding" (Romans 13:8) — to the philosophical wonderings of Ecclesiastes.

I also discovered the Bible doesn't say what I thought it did about money. For one thing, Scripture is not opposed to money itself. When Jesus told the rich, young ruler to give all he had to the poor (Matthew 19:16–24), it wasn't because Jesus hated wealth. It was because what got in the way of this young man's devotion to God was his love of money.

Over and over, the Bible warns us against pouring our soul into acquiring wealth. That's because running after it leads to chronic, spirit-sapping discontent. "Those who love money never have enough," the writer of Ecclesiastes says. "Those who love wealth are never satisfied with their income" (5:10).

The antidote for this life of discontent, says the writer, is to look to the source of all wealth to find blessing in what we have: "When God gives people wealth and possessions, and the ability to enjoy them, to accept their lot and be happy in their toil — this is a gift from God" (5:19).[1]

happy with what you have

When I first moved after having to sell my condo, I was reluctant to invite people into my new, much smaller apartment. But for my birthday last year, I invited some friends over for dessert. Imagine my surprise when they oohed and aahed over my simple furnishings.

As I looked at the denim slipcover on the ancient, cat-clawed couch, the colorful pillows I made myself, and the sun streaming through the windows, I thought, "Yes, I can be content with what I have in life — right now."

Living peacefully with what you have is a gift from God. It's a gift I hope to receive day by day for a long time.

They say that a journey of a thousand miles begins with one step. So to help me along, I've hung on my wall next to my desk a list of the debts I'd like to pay off in the next year. Normally, this would depress me. But near this sheet of paper I've also tacked up truths I've discovered that help assuage my deepest fears about money, such as "I'm a child of God," "I'll enjoy what I have every day," "I'm valuable," and "I'm free to give and to receive."

As I read these little slips of paper, I breathe a sigh of relief and whisper a prayer: "Amen, Lord, let these affirmations be so."[2]

Those who love money never have enough;
those who love wealth are never satisfied with their income.

Ecclesiastes 5:10

Money Myths

We all have deep-rooted attitudes about money, many of which rob us of happiness and peace of mind. What's worse, many of these assumptions are myths. Some of them include:

1. Money equals happiness. Who knows for sure that money doesn't bring happiness? Answer: people with loads of money. If your life outside the financial realm doesn't bring you more satisfaction than the idea of big bucks, you need to realign your thinking.

2. Money equals importance. God proved your worth by sacrificing for you the very life of his Son. The worth we find in material possessions is nothing compared to that sacrifice. Need a designer label? It's time for a true-value check.

3. Money equals fulfillment. It's not wrong to buy nice things for yourself or your family. But it's wrong to love those nice things so much that we go into debt for them and give them too much importance. Money isn't the root of all evil, but the love of money gets us into hot water every time (1 Timothy 6:10).

4. We own our possessions. We don't even own ourselves. God's Word says we're bought at a price, and we aren't our own (1 Corinthians 6:19–20). The real secret to contentment is recognizing God's ownership and giving him control. When we do that, we're set free from stewing over money.[3]

We should aim for balance and a godly perspective.

Because I pay the bills in our house, I was able to keep the credit card statements hidden from my husband, Chad. He didn't know how much debt we had until I confessed it to him out of overwhelming guilt.

A Spending Coach

I knew I couldn't go on like this.

I wanted to be like the woman in Proverbs 31:11, whose husband had "full confidence in her." But no matter what I tried, I wasn't strong enough to stop spending. My husband agreed to help by holding me accountable for every cent I spent.

I was surprised at how well this kept me in line. Before buying a new item, I thought, "I'm going to have to tell Chad about this, and he'll ask why I bought it when we already have so much stuff. And he'll be right."

My friend Shelah also had a problem with money. After God showed her that her spending habits showed a lack of stewardship, Shelah also looked for someone to keep her accountable. This spending coach now regularly asks Shelah a simple question: "Have you spent and saved your money in a way that pleases the Lord?"

Your spouse, a parent, or best friend can help you keep spending under control. When choosing an accountability partner, select someone who will:

• Understand how important it is for you to improve your spending habits and financial responsibility.

• Keep strictly confident your financial information.

• Be an encourager, not a critic.

• Ask you hard questions, such as, "Are you sure you didn't buy something that you haven't told me about?"

When I receive our next credit card statement in the mail, I know I can open it without dread. Only planned purchases will be on it, and we won't have any new debt that we can't pay off. I'll be able to show this statement to my husband without guilt. We'll stay within budget, and we might even have a little extra left over. What a great feeling![4]

tips on saving

There are many good reasons to save, the first of which is to be a good steward of what God has given you.

While Scripture is clear that our sense of security should be in God, not riches, it is also a biblical principle to work diligently and plan for the future. Consider the work ethics of ants, advises Proverbs 6:6. Ants never give up. They plan for winter all summer. They plan for summer all winter. And while they gather food for winter, they gather all they can.

Another reason to save is that our life expectancy is getting longer. Your retirement may last twenty to thirty years.

Then there's the peace of mind that comes with savings. With money put aside for emergencies, you don't have to panic when the roof starts leaking or the car sounds funny. If you struggle with saving, try these strategies:

1. Set goals. It helps to know what you hope to accomplish, so set long- and short-term goals. Do you want to buy a house? Retire at age fifty-five to become a missionary? Determine how much you need to save each month toward your goals.

2. Take full advantage of compounding. Most people don't realize the power of compounding—but King Solomon did. "He who gathers money little by little makes it grow," says Proverbs 13:11 NIV.

3. Take 10 percent off the top. If you have 10 percent of each paycheck directly deposited into your savings before receiving your check, you won't miss it. This also allows you to increase the amount you save as your income rises.

4. Max-it. Maximize automatic saving through payroll deductions. Taxes may be a fact of life but your part could be offset or deferred through 401(k)s, 403(b)s, IRAs, etc.

5. Keep your hands off savings. Don't make the mistake of borrowing against your retirement money, or your money will stop working for you. Studies show that people often borrow from their 401(k) when they're most vulnerable in their careers. If you don't pay that loan back quickly, it's considered a distribution on which you'll have to pay taxes and penalties.[5]

Our culture relentlessly tugs at the pockets of our children. They are bombarded with messages that tell them to buy the latest gadget, the coolest clothes, the hottest music.

lessons from an allowance

Increasingly, children buy into those messages. While it's always been important for us parents to teach our children to be wise in spending, we must also teach them how to be good stewards of their money.

The most obvious way to begin building good money habits in our children is to give them some money of their own and teach them to manage it. That's where allowances come in. Some families choose not to give allowances, but we've found a regular weekly allowance is an invaluable tool for instilling valuable lessons about tithing, saving, and spending.

We encouraged our boys to follow the guidelines recommended by many Christian financial planners: They must give 10 percent off the top to God, as Leviticus 27:30 advises, and live on the remaining amount.

Teaching children to be good stewards of their resources means helping them learn the difference between wants and needs. Once our sons had to live with their limited allowance, they quickly learned to adjust their spending.

Knowing how much money to give is the most difficult part of any allowance system. Honestly, there is no rule of thumb; you should give what seems reasonable to you, keeping in mind the cost of living in your area and how much you can afford to give.

No allowance system is perfect, but we've found a workable plan for us. Our kids are learning the difference between wants and needs and are discovering that being good caretakers of the financial gifts they've been given is an essential part of growing up with God. And that's the best lesson of all.[6]

Fun on a Budget

Having fun and spending money seem to go together, but you don't have to drop big bucks on a night out.

For couples who enjoy music, a local community orchestra or college music school offers great events at budget prices. In the college community near my home, a terrific orchestra gives free weekend concerts. A bookstore regularly hosts local jazz and folk musicians, many of whom are very good.

Choosing the times for entertainment can make a huge difference in the amount you spend. Mary Hunt and her husband, Harold, found ways to cut corners on dates without feeling deprived. "Instead of dinner and a movie, we go to a matinee, then out for coffee," Hunt says. "It makes a wonderful date at about half the cost."

For my husband, Jeff, and me, having a date can be as simple as driving to our favorite park for a long walk, then stopping somewhere for dessert and coffee. Checking out a free video at the library and microwaving a bag of popcorn provide the ingredients for some of our most enjoyable family nights.

If you have children who need a babysitter when you go on a date, consider trading nights a few times a month with another couple. With babysitters demanding higher prices all the time, swapping child-care services can save a lot of money.[7]

A single mother whose only income was child support once asked me how much she should tithe. Many of us struggle with the same question, regardless of our income.

How Much to Give

In the Old Testament, Moses taught the children of Israel to acknowledge that everything they had came from God by giving at least a tenth of it back to him. Tithing was an act of worship as well as obedience.

In Malachi 3:8–12, the prophet compares withholding the tithe to stealing from God. He urges people to give generously in order to experience God's blessing. God promises that if we honor him with our finances—no matter how difficult—he will honor us by providing for us in ways we can't begin to imagine.

In the New Testament, we're reminded that those who sow sparingly will also reap sparingly, but those who sow generously will reap generously (2 Corinthians 9:6). The apostle Paul adds, "Each of you should give what you have decided in your heart to give, not reluctantly or under compulsion, for God loves a cheerful giver" (9:7).

There are many ways to give besides money. Consider any special skills you have that might be used to bless others. Tithe your time to serve your church or community. Open your home to a Bible study group or make dinner for a visiting missionary couple. As 2 Corinthians 8:12 NIV says, "For if the willingness is there, the gift is acceptable according to what one has, not according to what he does not have."[8]

In the story of the widow's mite, Jesus reminds us that it's not the amount of the gift that matters to God—it's the attitude of the heart (Luke 21:1–4).

No one can serve two masters. Either you will hate the one and love the other, or you will be devoted to the one and despise the other. You cannot serve both God and money.

Matthew 6:24

Keep your lives free from the love of money and be content with what you have, because God has said, "Never will I leave you; never will I forsake you."

Hebrews 13:5

Starting Over

All my life I dreamed of having a man in my life to love me. I was involved in a few unhealthy relationships before I married a guy. I soon learned he had a problem with alcohol. When the marriage failed, I felt like a foreigner as a divorced, single parent in the Christian community. I felt unworthy, stained.

The story of Rahab (Joshua 2) gave me courage to start over. This prostitute hid two Israelite spies who came to Jericho. After Joshua and his people conquered Jericho, Rahab and her family went to live among the Israelites. She exchanged a life of sin for a life of faith, and she married a Hebrew. She soon gave birth to Boaz, securing her place in Christ's lineage (Matthew 1:5).

I've often wondered how Rahab felt as she walked out of Jericho to camp with the Israelites. She was a woman, a foreigner, and a former prostitute. Yet Hebrews 11:31 lists Rahab as a champion of faith. That gave me courage to believe I could have a second chance. I stopped worrying about what people thought of me.

My church family became to me like the Israelites were to Rahab. They welcomed my son and me, prayed for us, and loved us. God has used the body of Christ to help fill many of our needs. If God could take a sinner like Rahab and use her for his glory, he can do the same with me.[1]

Surviving a Breakup

Have you camped out in bed with a pint of Chunky Monkey ice cream and the TV remote? Are you thinking about buying a one-way ticket to an obscure Mediterranean island to live on the rest of your life?

Being left by the one you love has a way of making you a little loony. If you find yourself on the receiving end of romantic rejection, however, **the following suggestions will help you keep your sanity:**

1. Face reality. Getting dumped is difficult to accept. The notion of getting back together is a familiar theme for the jilted. Some part of our soul is convinced the other person feels the same way we do, only they don't know it yet. All of us have a hard time coming to terms with rejection, but we've got to face reality. Admit the relationship is over and move on.

2. Let yourself cry. A breakup is one of the toughest things you'll ever experience. It's heart wrenching, and you deserve to feel lousy. Breaking up from even an unhealthy relationship hurts. It's frightening to lose someone you loved and depended on. So give in to the agony and have a good cry. Scientific studies have shown that tears actually excrete depression-purging hormones. So you'll feel better physically and emotionally after a good cry.

3. Stop blaming yourself. While it's important to take a hard look at your behavior if you consistently make bad relationship choices, why punish yourself because you fell in love? Self-blame doesn't help you learn from mistakes and become a better person. Don't get caught in the guilt trap. Truth is, you aren't so powerful that you can cause someone else's behavior and choices. You can play a part in these decisions, but you can't cause them. You aren't to blame.

4. Go to God. You have a Father of compassion and a God of all comfort (2 Corinthians 1:3) to whom you can turn in situations like these. This may feel like small consolation at first, but if you keep leaning on God, you'll find he's more than enough.[2]

lessons of unemployment

My husband's extensive period of unemployment has highlighted God's abundant provision in our lives. For one, God has provided time: a season for our son Benjamin to be with his father. At age five, Benjamin may not consciously remember the details of this time, but it has shaped his character nonetheless.

During this time, my husband, Dennis, has read to his son, painstakingly taught him to play chess, showed him how to ride a bike without training wheels, and led him to master pinball and foosball. He has also modeled perseverance in action. Benjamin has learned from his dad how to weather disappointment, and how to pitch in and encourage others. And he has learned how to pray earnestly for a job for his father.

God's provision has also included a crash course in humility. When I had hand surgery, some friends brought over dinner and groceries. Later, we opened the card they'd included and found a generous gift certificate for the local supermarket. I expected my proud husband to refuse the gift, but instead he sat down at the kitchen table and wrote a heartfelt note of thanks.

I've been humbled as well. The other night I sat with a frozen smile as an acquaintance gushed about how her husband just was handed his dream job. I felt like the unloved stepsister in a fairy tale. As bitter tears wet my pillow that night, I became keenly aware of clean sheets, a full stomach, and a roof over my head. That night I committed to memory another lesson about provision: While what you have may not seem equitable compared to what others receive, you must trust God to give you exactly what you need.

I don't know whether we have weeks, months, or perhaps even years more to go in this trial. I don't know if we'll have to move away from a hometown we love so Dennis can find work. I don't know if there's a full-time career out there with my name on it. But when I dwell on all God has provided, I find the answers to questions I didn't know to ask.[3]

Expecting Too Much

Tom and Laura came to see us just nine months after their wedding. They had swallowed the happily-ever-after sugar pill whole and were now feeling queasy.

"Before we got married we couldn't bear to be apart," Laura said. "I thought we'd do even more things together once we were married. But now Tom says he needs space. He's not the guy I married."

Tom rolled his eyes, but Laura continued. "He used to be so considerate and thoughtful ..."

"Oh, and I'm a total slouch now?" Tom interrupted.

"Of course not. You—or maybe we—are just different now."

Nervously twisting his wedding band, Tom looked at Laura. "Marriage isn't what I expected, either. I thought you'd try to make life a little easier for me. Instead, when I come home from the office, all you want is to go out or ..."

"I make dinner for you every night," Laura said.

Silenced by their display of unrestrained emotion, the couple looked at us as if to say, "See! Our marriage isn't what it's supposed to be."

When they got married, Tom and Laura knew that marriage was hard work, but they didn't expect it to be a twenty-four-hour, seven-day-a-week job.

Plaguing every unsatisfied couple is a vast assortment of expectations about what marriage should be, juxtaposed with the reality of what marriage truly is. The expectations you bring to your partnership can make or break your marriage. Don't miss out on the best of marriage because your ideals are out of sync with reality. Instead, remember that the more open you are about your expectations, the more likely you and your spouse can help each other fulfill them.[4]

Making New Friends

I stood by the industrial-strength coffeepot, nervously juggling a Styrofoam cup of brew with my Bible and trying to make eye contact with potential friends in the adult Sunday school class.

Inside, I felt that intense aloneness that can grip you in a big crowd. Most of the fifty or so class members huddled in little groups, secure in their shared activities. However, I must have looked pathetic enough for one woman to break away and throw a morsel of conversation in my direction. "Is this your first Sunday here?" she asked.

I had been in the class for a year. And I still hadn't connected with anyone. Somehow, I hadn't figured out how to build relationships in a new place — and I was losing touch with my friends back home.

If you move a lot, you may shy away from making new friends because you're tired of investing in relationships, then packing your bags

again. So is friendship really worth the effort? Absolutely!

When a job change moved us again a year later, I was determined to make some changes. Like Scarlett O'Hara in *Gone with the Wind*, I vowed, "As God as my witness, I'll never be lonely again!" Okay, maybe that wasn't exactly what Scarlett said. But here are a few friendship lessons I've learned along the way:

1. Opposites can attract. Don't necessarily rule someone out because he's different than you.
2. Don't rule out someone because of age. You might miss a blessing.
3. Get involved in church. If you're a life-long Christian, this may

seem like a no-brainer. Yet, if you do what we did—attend church services and Sunday school without getting involved—you'll be a stranger to everyone.
4. Join a group. A great place to make friends is in a club or a group of people interested in the same things you are.
5. Try something new. The great thing about a move is being able to shake off everyone's expectations of who you are, and starting over. Always wanted to ski? Take some lessons. Thought about volunteering for Habitat for Humanity? Now's your opportunity. Chances are you'll meet some new friends along the way.[5]

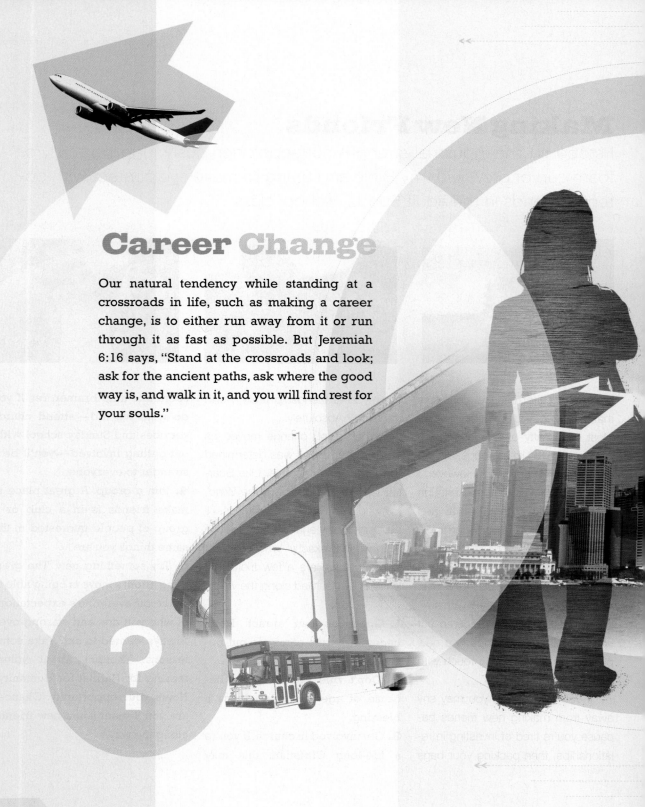

Career Change

Our natural tendency while standing at a crossroads in life, such as making a career change, is to either run away from it or run through it as fast as possible. But Jeremiah 6:16 says, "Stand at the crossroads and look; ask for the ancient paths, ask where the good way is, and walk in it, and you will find rest for your souls."

Notice the verbs in this verse: stand, look, ask, walk.

The first guiding principle when contemplating a career change is to stand and look. Take time to analyze yourself and your situation. Why do you want another career? Is the issue your job, or is it you? Do you want to make a change because workplace relationships seem askew? Does your boss behave badly? Are you behaving badly? How about workload—does it intrude on family time and make maintaining good relationships difficult?

Part of looking and asking is examining your responsibilities and skills. Are the things that you do best the same skills your employer needs? How about the level of challenge; do your responsibilities overwhelm or "underwhelm" you? Is the industry declining with more jobs being outsourced? Perhaps your family has grown and requires more money. Perhaps caring for aging parents necessitates more flexibility in work schedule.

Whatever the reason, make a list of your thoughts and needs and get input from others. Most important, bring the situation to God in prayer. As the Lord shows you the good way, walk in it. Trust and obey, even if it means not changing jobs.[6]

For this God is our God for ever and ever;
he will be our guide even to the end.

Psalm 48:14

super momism

I was an executive secretary for a pharmaceutical company. When I had two daughters, my drive to become the perfect working mother took root.

I figured if anyone could embody the essence of Super Mom while pursuing a career, it was me.

But I had trouble scaling the cliffs of Super Mom Summit while juggling the demands of the workplace. Eventually I let go of the dream of having it all at the same time and turned in my notice at work.

Those first few months at home were wonderful. I loved spending time with my kids. The more relaxed schedule allowed me to recuperate from all the pressures I'd put upon myself to be both the best worker in the world and Super Mom.

But it wasn't long before I realized there was something seriously wrong with the Super Mom I wanted to become. It's all well and good to strive for excellence in homemaking but watch out for the biggest threat many stay-at-home moms face: perfectionism in all the wrong places. In the rush to be perfect, our true aim gets lost in the shuffle, and our kids aren't any better off than before. Too much time fussing over clean closets and gourmet meals leaves us little time to enjoy our children or to forge the friendships that keep loneliness and imbalance at bay.

Six years into this, I've told Super Stay-at-Home Mom she can keep her stress and unrealistic expectations. In the meantime, I am learning to blend my realistic family plan with God's. The results — reflected in the faces of my children — look promising.[7]

Working from Home

Telecommuting (working from home) was challenging for me. Some mornings I lingered to finish one last thing, and the whole family had to scramble to get to the school bus on time. Other mornings my motivation flagged, and I had troubled getting out of bed.

Vicki, the babysitter, suggested I write Hebrews 12:11 on an index card. Crawling out of bed at 4 a.m., I repeated the verse to myself, "No discipline seems pleasant at the time, but painful. Later on, however, it produces a harvest of righteousness and peace for those who have been trained by it."

The benefits of working from home are abundant. My daughters share more of their lives with me than before, since I'm home when the day's events are fresh in their minds. We pray together over problems, and I have time to search God's Word for advice to give them. When my daughters are sick, I don't miss an entire day of work—I can log on and work while they're napping. My eldest daughter's math grades have improved because I have more time to help her study, and my younger daughter can now take an afternoon horseback riding class.

After two years of telecommuting, my coworkers are convinced I'm just as productive and responsive to problems as I was when I went in to work. My manager adopted a similar work pattern six months after me. She told me that my telecommuting experience inspired her to request the arrangement from her manager.

Working in a virtual office isn't for everyone. To be successful, you need the right kind of work, the right equipment, the discipline to work alone, and a receptive manager. But for many working moms, the effort is worth it.[8]

Trust in the LORD with all your heart
　　and lean not on your own understanding;
in all your ways submit to him,
　　and he will make your paths straight.

Proverbs 3: 5–6

late-in-life pregnancy

Jamie and Eric met as freshman in college and were married after their sophomore year. Working full-time and planning to complete their degrees, their lives were full and their marriage happy. The only thing they hadn't planned for was a baby. So how did they cope with the unexpected pregnancy?

Jamie: We had been married only four months when I found out I was pregnant. I was really excited but anxious at the same time. There were many lifestyle changes that we knew were coming. I was planning to go back to school and finish up my degree. I knew I'd have to give up some of those goals now that I was pregnant.

Eric: Since we hadn't thought about this kind of situation beforehand, there was a lot of financial anxiety. It was tough enough to figure out our finances after we got married, and we knew it would only be harder with a child.

Jamie: We had to work out a new way to make our schooling and jobs work in this new situation. Before, we had decided that I would start school while Eric worked. Then we'd switch. But with the baby on the way, that had to be rearranged.

Jamie: We were also faced with the challenge of becoming what we wanted our child to learn, since we knew that our actions would speak louder than our words. When we started working through these issues, the pregnancy pushed us as a couple to become more mature.

Eric: Preparing for a baby steadied our marriage. We made a commitment to work through issues that came up because we wanted to get our act together. We never looked at the situation as though it was the end of the world. Instead, we've always considered it a blessing.[9]

Chapter Ten

Personal Growth

follow your calling

It's an amazing and fulfilling thing to live in line with God's design and calling on your life. But sometimes it's difficult and overwhelming to discover what that is. My suggestion? Pay attention to how God made you. What gives you energy? What are you good at? What do you love to do? What patterns in your life may be clues to your design and calling?

Before he met Christ, the apostle Paul was an activist and a zealot. He was also an opponent of the church. After he met Christ, Paul continued to be an activist and a zealot, but he changed his allegiance. Acts 9:20 says Paul at once began to preach in the synagogues that Jesus is the Son of God. He didn't change who he was by design, but he did change the Lordship in his life.

God's calling for your life goes way beyond what you do. It's who you are, where you belong, whom you love, and how you love. In our culture's preoccupation with success and celebrity, it's easy to approach one's calling in a way that's not much more than success and celebrity covered by a thin veneer of spirituality.

Parker Palmer wrote a wonderful book *Let Your Life Speak*, which shows us how to discover and live a life in which our God-given design intersects with what the world needs. When we operate with the gifts God has given us and are mindful of meeting the needs of others, we have a life that beautifully reflects the person of God. The world could use more people like that.[1]

hope after addiction

I began the hard work of breaking my addiction to alcohol when I called a counselor and asked for help. He suggested a support group for my husband and me and eventually guided us through the process of asking a few friends for support and prayer.

Without a doubt, contacting a pastor, counselor, support group, or friend and whispering those life-changing words, "I need help," is the beginning of change.

I found breaking the bondage of addiction requires three things the apostle Paul describes as the foundation for Christian living: faith, hope, and love (1 Corinthians 13:13). Specifically, that means:

1. Viewing the past through the lens of faith. As I faced some painful experiences in my past, I recognized I had tried to overcome a disappointing world with perfection and performance. I began to understand the feelings I had tried to numb with alcohol. And I saw the forgiveness God offered to me. Ultimately the past is redeemed when you can say with the apostle Paul, "Who will rescue me from this body of death? Thanks be to God ... through Jesus Christ our Lord!" (Romans 7:24–25). I'm grateful for what alcoholism has taught me about God's grace, love, and forgiveness.

2. Viewing the present in the light of God's love. The more we accept God's forgiveness and unconditional love, the less powerful addiction becomes. Out of God's unconditional love for us is his call to love others as we love ourselves (Romans 13:9). Part of loving ourselves is paying attention to physical health. I can't stress enough the importance of physical exercise. Addiction works against the body's ability to produce and disperse endorphins (chemicals that produce a feeling of well-being). Over time, regular exercise helps restore the process.

3. Viewing the future with hope. Women with an addiction are usually trying to experience a level of perfection and joy that can be found only in heaven. Understanding that those longings will be met only in eternity with God helps us wait with a fresh hope. And having confidence in this future hope frees us to dream and plan our days on earth.[2]

A Bad Image

I turned the pages of my college alumni magazine with trepidation, reading about classmates who had become doctors, lawyers, entrepreneurs, artists, and politicians. "You're just a mom," I thought as I slumped into depression.

Others are world-changers; I'm a diaper-changer. They're enforcing policies to save the environment; I'm enforcing policies to save my carpet. It's easy to lack confidence when I slip into that trap of comparison. I decided to put my magazine down and turn to the Bible. Paul's words in the first few paragraphs of 2 Timothy

were heart wrenching. Many people in the church were ashamed of Paul, nearly everyone in Asia had deserted him, and only one visitor came to see him in prison: Onesiphorus. The great apostle was sidelined and forgotten by nearly everybody. In the closing paragraphs of 2 Timothy, Paul cries out in desperation to Timothy: "When you come, bring the cloak that I left . . . and my scrolls. . . . Do your best to get here before winter". (4:13, 21).

Yet it was under those strenuous circumstances that Paul wrote his inspired letters to Timothy. Even in

prison Paul didn't lose his vision to serve as an instrument for noble purposes.

Do we remember the man who sentenced Paul to prison? Do we remember all the powerful, successful leaders of his day? No. But all around the world and through the years since, countless lives have been transformed by the faithful words of a lowly prisoner who described himself as having "finished the race" (4:7).[3]

What patterns in your life may be clues to your design and calling?

balancing work and family

If you're currently trying to determine what mix of work and family is right for you, **do this little home-work assignment:**

1. Define what it means to stay at home. My children attended day care or preschool twelve to fifteen hours a week from the time they were three months old, but I considered myself a stay-at-home mother. Other working moms I know run their home business after their children go to bed, juggle schedules with their husband, or split part-time work between their home and an office. Some fit the traditional picture of a homemaker. What would be ideal for you?

2. Live on one income. Children bring increased expenses, making it difficult to cut back on your lifestyle after they've arrived. Learn to live on one income before they come, and put the other income into savings. My husband and I did this when we first married, and we can testify that it's doable. The savings also come in handy when you buy a house, a car, or plan a vacation.

3. Calculate what it costs to work. Figure the cost of wardrobe, transportation, day care, lunches out, cleaning services, and whatever else you might spend going to work. Then calculate the after-tax pay you'll actually bring home. My sister-in-law figured out that after expenses, she'd be making about fifty cents an hour.

4. Decide what role you want to play in your child's life. I avoided returning to an office environment once my children were in school because I wanted to be available to them. Many women plan to return to the work force as soon as their youngest child reaches kindergarten, only to find their desire to be available to their children goes up.

5. Find your self-worth in God. If you currently find great fulfillment in your career but are considering staying home, don't wait until you're home to have a ready answer to the question, "What do you do?" Be clear on why you made the choices you did. Before you leave the workplace, tell yourself that God values you, not because of what you do but because you're his child.[4]

Double Duty at Home

I've never felt guilty for trading my pantyhose and pumps for jeans and sneakers to work from home. I love being a full-time mom. I'm on call twenty-four hours a day, seven days a week. I get no vacation, no sick days, no personal time off. Work requires a strong command of my native language, consistent organization, and skillful diplomacy. Strength training is a plus.

But as I try to reconcile the needs of my two jobs in a twenty-hour day—one for pay and the other for love—I need to be reminded that this double duty is for a good reason. I'm discovering my family-room office is no less a mission field than the streets of Calcutta. I know God has called me to my current vocation because of the people I meet along the path, such as the client with whom I shared my faith because he was intrigued by my volunteer work at my church.

Working mostly from home, I talk to people more through email than in person. Except for occasional meetings, I rarely leave my home office. That doesn't mean God uses me any less. I cling to the same thing Jesus' disciples embraced. While their vocation—fishing—wasn't glamorous, Christ used their work to shape them into people he could use in other, more life-changing labor. They learned, as I'm learning, that what we do, who we are, and where we live are not by coincidence.[5]

Overcoming Jealousy

I wasn't jealous, of course; merely, uh, competitive. I recognized the ugly truth of my jealousy one gray morning when I received an announcement from a colleague who had received an opportunity that I was convinced should have been mine.

I tossed the letter across the room in a huff, whining, "It's not fair, Lord!"

He seemed to respond: "Was the cross of Calvary fair, Liz? Have I called you to succeed — or surrender?" I was undone. Jealousy, envy, and strife were alive and well in my heart. After a time of weeping and confession, I knew what had to happen next. I sent a heartfelt memo to more than sixty peers in writing and speaking, confessing to these women who love and serve the Lord that they pushed my jealousy button without their even knowing it. I invited them to respond (anonymously, of course) to a survey on jealousy so that we might all learn how to deal with the seldom-discussed reality of professional jealousy.

Their candid responses began pouring in. I was especially touched by one leader who wrote, "I could be really spiritual, but I'll be truthful instead."

Comparisons are never productive unless Christ is the mirror. He is the one who is "jealous" for us before God, who wants our whole heart, mind, body, and soul to be focused on him rather than others.

A friend who admitted to once being a nine on the jealousy scale is now happily living at a one. "The more we hear God's voice and are settled in what he is calling us to do, the less we are vulnerable to envy and jealousy," she says. "If we keep a grateful heart, we can rejoice when others succeed!"[6]

Controlling Anger

Some things in life warrant anger. But God cautions us in Ephesians 4:26 not to let anger give way to sin. In other words, it's not anger that's sinful but what we do after we become angry.

We need to respond in a way that brings positive resolution. And we need to be more discriminating about what provokes our anger. Too often anger springs from small irritants — forgetful spouses, distracted drivers, inconsiderate coworkers, cranky children — none of which warrants the energy that anger wastes or the control it assumes over us.

While there was a legitimate basis for my anger that night we lost power (it wasn't the first time I'd dealt with Steve's lackadaisical attention to basic details such as paying the electric bill), my anger was way out of proportion to the offense. It was clear that I wasn't interested in resolution; I wanted revenge!

Disproportionate anger makes resolution difficult, if not impossible. I was once on a civic committee with several people, and one of the members was habitually late to our meetings. Tardiness was a huge irritant to the chairman. She wasn't wrong to expect everyone to be on time, but her explosive anger against the latecomer became a greater problem. Eventually she was replaced as chairman.

For anger to have healthy results, it needs to be reasonable and under control so you can approach the person who provoked your anger in a way that will let him hear what you're saying and make the necessary adjustments.[7]

The more I become aware of the danger of self-absorption, the more I see things in me I don't care for. Maybe it's buying something I can afford but don't really need. I am practicing saying no to myself.

My Sinful Past

Show me your ways, LORD,
    teach me your paths.
Guide me in your truth and teach me,
    for you are God my Savior,
    and my hope is in you all day long.

Psalm 25:4–5

You need to persevere so that when you have done the will of God, you will receive what he has promised.

Hebrews 10:36

The Lord is also showing me the importance of tuning in to what's going on in the lives of oppressed people around the world. I pray daily to keep from being too family centered when there's a big world out there. I can implode with self-absorption if I'm not careful.

One of the most wonderful things God has done for me is to leave intact memories of my miserable past. I'd be an idiot to think highly of myself after where I've been. The very thing I hate the most is the thing that protects me from pride.

I struggle with this, though. One time, a pastor who became aware of my sinful past decided I wasn't appropriate to lead his women's group. That broke my heart, but I bowed to it. If what you need is a sparkling clean testimony, you're not going to get it from me. But if you could use a testimony that there's life after pit dwelling, then maybe I can be your girl.

I'm ashamed of my sins, but all I can do now is walk in the Holy Spirit's power. That is my life's pursuit till I see Jesus face-to-face.[6]

Chapter Eleven

Love and Friendship

Two are better than one,
    because they have a good return for their labor:
If they fall down,
    they can help each other up.

Ecclesiastes 4: 9 – 10

communication breakdown

The argument started when we were thumbing through a magazine and saw a photo of a supercool stackable washer and dryer depicted in a spotless laundry room. "Why can't our laundry room look like that?" asked Les.

I stiffened. This wasn't the first time we'd covered this ground. Throughout our marriage we've tossed the chore of washing laundry back and forth. But recently it's been my responsibility, and with two little boys it was becoming more of a challenge. "If you want to do the laundry, be my guest," I snapped.

With that, we were off and running. If you were eavesdropping, you would never have known that we were on our way home from leading a marriage seminar. We weren't even close to practicing what we preach.

We finally resorted to a strategy we've developed for just such an occasion. We got out our reminder of what's truly important in communication. It's only one sentence: "Seek to understand before being understood."

This simple thought, popularized by Stephen Covey in *Seven Habits of Highly Effective People*, inevitably gets us back on track. It sounds simple, but it's profound. And it works. Once you try to understand your partner before you try to get him or her to understand you, your communication skills, no matter how rudimentary, take a quantum leap.

After thinking about that sentence, I relaxed my defenses and tried to understand Les's perspective. "You really value having an or-

ganized and orderly life. Sometimes I forget how much that means to you," I said. I could barely believe those words were coming out of my mouth!

Les recognized my sincerity and acknowledged the struggle to keep up with our growing family. Our entire conversation turned around. We were able to get back on track with a civilized and constructive dialogue.

So take it from a couple of very human relationship experts: the next time you find yourselves stepping on each other's toes, try a new step. Clarify content and seek understanding.[1]

Peace in Forgiveness

At a conference several years ago, I was talking to a woman who'd been physically abused throughout her marriage. She was now divorced, but she still was having trouble forgiving her ex-husband. I explained that in the Bible the word for forgiveness means to abandon, to send away, leave alone.

True forgiveness is a releasing. I don't have to wait to forgive until I feel like forgiving. That may never happen. Instead, I must choose to forgive. God will deal with whatever else needs to be done.

When someone first shared that insight with me, I felt a tremendous sense of relief. As I passed it on to this new divorcee, her eyes filled with tears. She realized forgiving her ex-husband didn't mean condoning his behavior; it meant releasing him and letting God deal with him.

Ordinary annoyances, such as when your spouse interrupts you during a conversation or forgets to pay a bill, can cause friction in marriage. These small irritations can grow into mountains if they're not dealt with. But if we make forgiveness a habit, even for little things, it will be much easier to forgive the big ones.

Anger is toxic. If we don't take care of it, it can turn inward and become bitterness. That takes a toll on us psychologically and physically. It causes undue stress and physical issues.

The apostle Paul says, "In your anger do not sin. Do not let the sun go down while you are still angry" (Ephesians 4:26). God didn't design our bodies to carry the venom of anger and bitterness. He designed us to live in peace and harmony with our mates, which can only occur through forgiveness.[2]

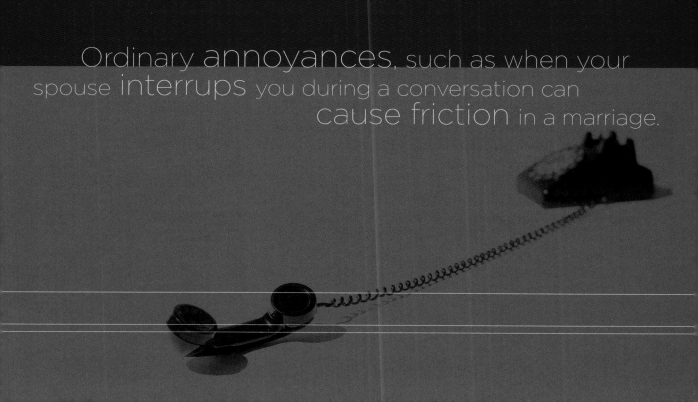

Ordinary annoyances, such as when your spouse interrups you during a conversation can cause friction in a marriage.

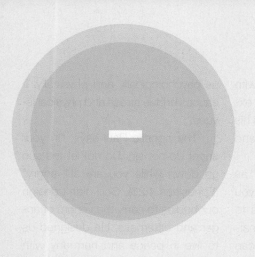

Appreciating Differences

Kay and I were virtual strangers when we got married, but we began finding out things about each other immediately, such as realizing that apart from our love for God, we were about as opposite as two people could be. We viewed life from different angles and argued about everything.

Kay's father sat us down the night before we were married and said, "There are five areas where marriages usually have conflict: money, sex, in-laws, children, and communication." He was prophetic: Kay and I fought over every one of those items.

Not only did we disagree over those things, we couldn't even agree about how to disagree. Kay is an intense person who needs to talk. My preferred method of dealing with problems is just to walk away. That is a volatile combination.

The single factor that kept us married in those early years was that we agreed on one thing: divorce would never be an option for us. You can't leave the door open to that even a little bit, or eventually one of you will try to escape. Because we knew we were in it for the long haul, we were forced to accept each other's differences. What else could we do?

Slowly, over time, God helped us to accept our differences and to appreciate them. Through the process we learned that any successful marriage is built upon the biblical truth that God designed each of us with five purposes in mind: worship, fellowship, discipleship, ministry, and missions.

Until you realize you were placed here for God's purposes, your life and your marriage will be difficult, complicated, and exhausting. But once you understand God's plan, your life and your marriage take on new meaning.[3]

finding mr. right

Until a few years ago, I shopped for men like I shop for Kleenex or jelly beans — with a list. A girl knows what she's getting when she makes a list. She can size up her date and compare him with the list to make sure he's worthy.

Some of my criteria were valid — he must love God and me. Others were a tad lofty. For example, at one point, my goal was to marry a man who looked like Mel Gibson, was as sensitive as my closest girlfriend, and as wise as Jesus. He had to be funny, financially stable, athletic, charismatic, good with children, patient, a good communicator, gentle, and assertive. He had to share my life's vision and balance his checkbook. He couldn't have a hair on his back, a spare tire around his middle, or live in a trailer.

I couldn't find a man to meet these criteria. By age thirty-three, I was shopped out. A friend gave me a journal for my birthday with Colossians 3:14 on the cover: "And over all these virtues put on love, which binds them all together in perfect unity." I asked God what he wanted me to learn from this verse, and I sensed him whisper, "Shana, love is the bond of perfection; perfection isn't the bond of perfection."

Suddenly I realized the error of my thinking. I had thought that if I found the perfect mate, I'd have the perfect love. But God says that perfection doesn't create a perfect bond; God-honoring love, even in the midst of imperfection, does.

I realize ditching my list doesn't mean giving up all my standards; it means adopting God's higher, better standards. This means looking for a man who shares my faith and who exhibits patience, gentleness, humility, generosity, and kindness. These qualities never will steer a girl wrong.

Ditching my list also means being open to the mysterious, unpredictable nature of love, and being focused on believing God knows what I need in romantic relationships. I trust his judgment more than mine any day![4]

searching for love

Q. I'm twenty-five and single. I love the Lord. Lately I've been confused about how to find the right partner. In my church, dating is viewed almost as a sin. People believe in the praying method—that God will show you the right person when he's ready. What is the right way to find the partner God has for me?

A. The way your church is telling people to seek a mate reminds me of the joke about a man clinging to his rooftop during a flood. He prays that God will send him deliverance. Pretty soon a man in a rowboat comes by. "No thanks," the man on the rooftop says, "I'm waiting on God to save me." Later a family paddles up to him on a raft, and finally a helicopter drops him a rope ladder, but the man waves them all off. Finally, water comes over the rooftop, and the man drowns.

He finds himself standing before God's throne. "I prayed to you, Lord," he protests. "Why didn't you save me?"

"I sent you a rowboat, a raft, and a helicopter," the Lord replies. "What were you waiting for?" It sounds like your church is telling people to expect a miraculous sign to direct you to a mate rather than using more ordinary means. God has given us his Word, your own intelligence, friends, family, and other believers. All these elements can work together when we are praying for discernment in finding a mate.

The first step, then, is to ask God to guide you. Then keep your eyes open for that raft or rowboat. Perhaps a young man keeps coming to mind, and you wish you knew him better.

The second step is to use your intelligence. Does this young man seem like a companion for your life journey? Would he help you put God first? Would he want you to love God more than himself?

Third, get the advice of other Christians whom you respect. Ask family and friends whether they think this is a match worth pursuing. Ask clergy and elders at the church as well; it is always good to get the perspective of an older generation that has seen many marriages at work. Gather opinions and weigh them alongside your own inclinations. Then act on the advice.[5]

Hi!

Hello

Keeping in Touch

We women are on the move. Jobs, ministry opportunities, and family commitments often draw us to new locations. And while moving can be exciting, leaving dear friends behind is not.

How do you keep in touch with good friends? Check out this advice from other women with long-distance buddies:

My friend and I live three hours apart. For ten years we've set aside one Saturday in November to be our day. We meet at a small mall that's about half the distance for each of us. We shop, but our primary purpose is to catch up on each other's lives without children or husbands in tow and get renewed by each other's company.
—**Beth Troop, Pennsylvania**

Six friends and I became close during our single years. When we married, started moving out of state, and began raising families, we decided we didn't want to give up our friendship. So when our children grew old enough to travel easily, our families (seven dads, seven moms,

seven boys, and seven girls) chose a weekend when we could vacation together.

During that weekend, we enjoyed family time as well as mommies-alone and daddies-alone time. We even held our own church service. We created some wonderful memories and hope to do another weekend next year.
—**Katy Mount, Arizona**

With unlimited long-distance phone service, my family, friends, and I can do things "together-separately," as we call it. Sometimes I watch a favorite television show together-separately over the phone with my sister. And just yesterday, I had afternoon tea together-separately with a dear friend. We love this means of sharing moments across the miles.
—**Lucy Akard Seay, Michigan**

My friends and I belong to a blog ring. We each journal on the blog. We can read about our struggles and joys and leave encouraging comments for each other. It's like meeting for coffee each day, only thousands of miles apart.
—**MeLissa Houdmann, Colorado**

A year ago, I sent my friend, who had just moved out of state, a subscription to a devotional. Soon she asked if we could do a more in-depth study. I was thrilled. She and I had read the Bible together as teens, but over the years she had drifted from her Christian roots. Now, every Sunday night we have a Bible study by phone. Our friendship has always been a special bond, but now it's bound together by the love of Jesus.[6]
—**Kathy Esqueda, California**

friends at work

As women who spend many of our waking hours at an office or volunteering in some capacity, it's natural for us to be on the lookout for friends.

But who is that woman in the cubicle, classroom, or seat next to us? How can we tell whether she's someone we can trust to become a true friend? Some questions to ask:

1. Is she respectful of the truth? Maybe I'm more trusting than most, but I didn't realize the importance of asking this question until a new friend spread lies about me.

2. Will she keep a private matter private? Friendship grows through the intimate sharing of joys and sorrows that aren't for the whole world to know. In the Old Testament, wise King Solomon said, "Gossips separate close friends" (Proverbs 16:28).

3. Will she act without jealousy? It's hard to find anyone who doesn't carry a personal agenda of one kind or another. Someone who holds our best interests at heart is a friend to be valued.

4. Will she challenge me toward excellence? I had a friend at work who complained all the time. We worked side by side, and frankly our jobs warranted every grievance she voiced. It didn't take long for me to pick up her habit. I still recall the day when we met in the ladies room and traded frustrations. Unknown to us, our boss was eavesdropping on us.

If it's true a friend can tear us down, it's also true that the right friend can build us up. Choose your friends wisely, and pick up their good habits, not their bad.[7]

Confronting a Friend

Because relationships involve flawed people who make mistakes and get into messes, friends are needed not just for fun and affirmation, but also for words of instruction and correction. Committing to a friendship means that we care so deeply about someone that we have the courage to speak up when that person needs to hear tough words of truth.

Before addressing a difficult situation with a friend, though, examine your motives. If you have any self-righteousness, feelings of one-upmanship, even the tiniest desire to get even for something this friend has said to you, then you should keep silent, at least for a time. Honesty in touchy matters must be accompanied by pure, loving motives. If your words aren't bathed in love, they'll hurt rather than heal. Speaking honestly with a friend about a serious matter requires that we put thought and planning into our words. That means tuning in to how our friend is responding to what we say.

When you need to confront your friend about something, begin with prayer. Ask God to give you the right words and to take away wrong motives. Select a time when you and your friend will have privacy and won't be interrupted. Begin by affirming your love and care for your friend. Then, calmly and gently, say what you've observed. Take care not to pass judgment or blame.

Your friend may become defensive, angry, or hurt. Match your words to her response. If she is open, talk in greater depth about your concerns. If she clams up, back off. Remind her how much you care about her, and tell her that if she feels like talking about the situation some other time, you'll be there for her. Give her a hug, tell her you're praying for her, and change the subject.

True friendships are a blessing from God. Starting today, be honest with your friends about how much they mean to you, how much you treasure your time together, and how much you value your relationship with them.[8]

Friends and Mentors

I was a tomboy growing up, so most of my friends were guys. It wasn't until I became a speaker for Women of Faith conferences—along with Barbara Johnson, Patsy Clairmont, Thelma Wells, Marilyn Meberg, and Luci Swindoll—that I finally gained the kind of female friends for which I'd secretly longed.

After several years of traveling and sharing a stage together, we speakers have become close friends. As the youngest group member, I've learned valuable lessons from these dynamic women of God.

Luci has taught me to celebrate life's little moments. For example, when we arrived early at one year's first Women of Faith conference to familiarize ourselves with our new stage setup, nothing was ready. Everyone except Luci stared at each other. But Luci said, "Let's have a party!" What could have been a lost day turned out to be awesome, thanks to Luci.

Barbara is an amazing conduit of God's love. She is a great listener. When people are hurting, she just listens and weeps with them. That's a stark contrast to how I've handled hurting people in the past.

Thelma is a prime example of the what-you-take-in-is-what-you-give-out theory. I used to wonder how Thelma always had the right Scrip-

ture verse to share at the right moment. Then I realized she's never without her Bible. She's always taking in biblical truths, so she always has them to give out.

Patsy has taught me to tune in to others. Although she's spunky onstage, she's introspective off. But even while she's quiet, she's paying attention to others. She looks past her pain to attend to yours.

Marilyn is a beautiful example of unconditional love. No matter what I've done, she still loves me. I feel safe with her. When everything else in my life is going crazy, I can unload on Marilyn. I want to offer that kind of love and support to others.

I need these dear friends to help me become the kind of woman I want to be. It won't happen on my own. I'll always have solitary tendencies, especially when my old enemy, depression, tries to creep back into my life. While my first reaction is to pull away from others, I now have friends who constantly check in with me. What a privilege.[9]

> Anyone who withholds kindness from a friend
> forsakes the fear of the Almighty.
>
> Job 6:14

letting others help

I was never so tired in my life. My husband, Ben, had ruptured a disc in his lower back, forcing him to lie on the floor for six weeks while I tended to him, a three-year-old, and a crawling baby.

Every wail or jostle from the children sent Ben into spasms of pain, so I was constantly on edge. Preparing meals, mowing the lawn, changing diapers, and managing visitors left me bone weary and dull. It seemed that every day would be more of the same.

Answering a knock on the door one day, I saw my friend Roxanne armed with buckets, cleansers, and rubber gloves.

"Oh, no!" I thought, "of all people!" The picture of elegant grace, Roxanne was someone I hoped to be like someday. But cleaning my house was not what I pictured her doing.

"Come in," I stammered, then gulped as I envisioned her discovering the biosphere growing in my bathrooms.

What a lesson in humility I received that day. I have rarely been encouraged by the body of Christ as I was when Roxanne cleaned my toilets.

Sometimes holding unswervingly to the hope we profess means letting go of the pride that keeps other Christians at a distance. Let the body of Christ minister to you at your point of need. As people come together in service, the fragrance of Christ comes close as well. We're reminded we are not alone. We are free to hope.[10]

Chapter Twelve

Family

sister love

When people live up-close-and-personal with you for years, they get to know the real you. My sisters know I'm bossy, have tunnel vision, and am a stress-aholic. I don't have to explain all that before we get on with our friendship. And they love me anyway.

Adele and I, especially, have grown together; we know the worst about each other, and we're still the best of friends. We've prayed each other through childbirth, baby's fevers, illnesses, and other daily dilemmas.

The great thing about Adele is that I'll call for something simple, like Aunt Konnie's chili recipe, and in no time flat we're talking about things that really matter, such as family problems and spiritual struggles. Adele is a great blessing to me. Spiritual things are as immediate and real to her as creating lesson plans for home-schooling her daughter Emily.

Just after her second daughter was born, Adele wrote, "I had secretly hoped this baby would be a girl. Because of our friendship, I wanted so much for Emily to have a sister." I cried.

My sister Dawn and I love to remember how, when we were kids, I used to lie on the floor with my nose in whatever novel I couldn't put down and she'd sit on my back and do my hair. As it turned out, I became a journalist, and she became a beautician.

We've been in each other's hair ever since. That's fine with us, because it's a great feeling to know that even in a world of change, nothing really changes with us.[1]

Worrying about the Kids

Q. I constantly worry about my two kids. Sometimes I lie awake at night thinking about all the things that could harm them. Praying about my concerns doesn't seem to ease my mind. Any suggestions?

A. I remember when I experienced similar feelings. I not only worried about my children's physical safety but also about their spiritual safety in the midst of an ungodly culture. God taught me an important lesson that applies to both of those fears.

I was at my church's midweek prayer service when I, along with many others, stood to indicate that I had a special prayer need. I wanted God to protect my children because I was growing increasingly afraid for them, and that worry was out of control. The older my children became, the more I felt them slip from my protective grasp.

The moment I stood to my feet, 2 Timothy 1:12 popped into my mind: "I know whom I have believed, and am convinced that he is able to guard what I have entrusted to him for that day."

I realized that the Lord was telling me that while I could not adequately protect my kids, he could. What I needed to do was commit those children to him every day, then trust him.

I know that God is more than able to take care of my children. You know that, too. So hand your kids over to the only hands in which they'll truly be safe.[2]

the first year of parenting

When my husband, Jim, and I were new parents, we would hit the wall of exhaustion around 8 p.m. That's when we'd finally get our sweet little Emily to bed and start what magazines refer to as couple time. For us, couple time consisted of figuring out who had the energy to get plates out of the cupboard so we could eat a real meal, and who would pick up Emily's trail of books, toys, and assorted shoes (she was really into shoes).

Before long, we'd drag ourselves off to bed. As we turned out the lights and began fading into dreamland, we'd look at each other and say, "Isn't she wonderful?"

People tend to think of the first year of parenting as a fraternity hazing, a trial you must overcome before you can join the ranks of real parents. Near the end of my pregnancy, other mothers felt the need to tell me all the difficult parts of having a baby: the lack of sleep, the mess, the stress, the absence of a sex life. Their intent was to prepare me for the rough road ahead.

But nobody told me how amazing that first year is.

No one told me that watching a child grow and change is one of God's greatest gifts. Even if they had, I don't think I could have grasped what they meant. Really, there aren't enough words to describe what it feels like to be a parent or to wholly explain the wonder of the first year.

The other night, Jim and I were talking about Emily, like we usually do. He asked me, "What's been the best part of being a mom?"

I thought awhile, then answered, "It's watching another person become."

Think about it: in every other relationship, we meet a person at some point along their journey through life. My friends are people I met when we were eight or nineteen or twenty-seven. We know only parts of each other's lives.

Even the most intimate relationships start in the midst of a life being lived. I met Jim when he had a good twenty-four years under his belt. I met my parents when they were a third of the way into their lives. But with our children, we are there from the get-go. We are there for all the firsts, for the moments that shape them, for the most amazing changes of their entire lives.[3]

Honoring In-Laws

Honoring parents is a concept so important to God that he included it on his top-ten list of rules for living. Early in our life together, Chad and I took God's divine directive to cultivate attitudes and actions that honored each other's parents. But we were brand new to this task. How could we balance our desire to honor them while establishing ourselves as a separate family?

We discovered that honoring your in-laws has nothing to do with whether you like them, get along with them, or feel like honoring them. Honoring them needs to be done out of obedience to God and, hopefully, blessing will follow. As Ephesians 6:2–3 says: "Honor your father and mother"—which is the first commandment with a promise—"so that it may go well with you and that you may enjoy long life on the earth."

When I asked my mom about her motivation for nurturing her relationship with her mother-in-law (my paternal grandmother), she said, "I do it because I want to do the right thing." She didn't say, "I do it because I want to." Feelings, which change from day to day, are not the criteria for obeying God, "who does not change like shifting shadows." (James 1:17).

The night Chad suggested we invite his parents along on a movie date, I didn't particularly feel like including them. We had seen them earlier that day at a wedding reception, and I was looking forward to time alone with Chad. "I really think it would mean a lot to my parents if we asked them," Chad said. I was faced with an "honoring moment." Had I based my decision on what I felt like doing, I would have refused to go along with his idea. But when I factored in the spiritual value of obeying God by doing something that pleases him, my feelings ceased to be the determining factor.

"It means so much to a parent when their grown children want to spend time with them," my mother-in-law wrote in a note several days after our double date. I knew our time together had been not merely a pleasant diversion but an occasion of honor.[4]

It means so much to a parent when there grown children want to spend time with them

nurturing a child's faith

As parents, we want so much for our children to know and love God that we often become anxious that we aren't doing enough to build a spiritual foundation in their lives. But in truth, our children are just beginning their journey of experiencing God. The Bible says there is a season for everything (Ecclesiastes 3), and that includes your child's ever-growing relationship with God.

Still, this is a wonderful time to help that relationship begin. Young children are spiritual people who are particularly open to the wonder and mystery of God. They are at a stage where they are just discovering the concept of personhood, of recognizing that they are separate from you and can think and do things on their own. This helps them understand God as a real person whom they can talk to and who cares about them.

One of the best ways to reinforce this concept of God is to teach children how to pray. Prayer is about knowing and trusting God. It's engaging for children, readily connects to their interests and experiences, and can be learned and practiced in a variety of ways. Prayer also opens the door to all kinds of conversations about God.

When you pray with your children, remind them that God is with us all the time and prayer connects us with God at any time wherever we are. Pray often and in a variety of places to show your child that prayer is not just something we do at bedtime or before meals. Pray in the sandbox, in the bathtub, or in the car. Pray when your child feels afraid or when he's excited. Pray for other family members and friends.

The development of faith is different from other kinds of development. It's not just about facts and information. It's a multidimensional, life-altering process that infiltrates every part of our being. Trust that God can build a bright flame from the sparks of faith that you're lighting in your child.[5]

Sonja and I had been married for five years and had no children. That was an immediate red flag to nosy people we met at church.

Divinely Designed Family

"Don't you know that children are a gift from God?" one man asked, not knowing that Sonja and I had asked God most every day for five years to bless us with a child.

"You'd better get started!" some would say. That would launch us into a conversation about how we'd been trying to conceive without success. The response, "At least you're having fun trying, right?" usually came with a wink.

We were not having fun trying. When you're infertile, making love takes on the not-so-romantic air of an assembly line production, where the baby factory yields nothing month after month, year after year. Trying to get pregnant isn't fun when you're stringing together seventy-two months of mandatory sex and failing to conceive.

In all their testing, doctors found no reasons to explain our inability to conceive. We were young, Sonja ovulated normally and had no conditions that would

preclude conception, and my sperm was grade A. Yet we were unable to do what all those people with unwanted pregnancies could do: conceive. With straight faces, medical experts diagnosed our condition as "Unexplained Infertility." Brilliant. Now I know why my faith isn't in science.

In time Sonja and I decided to submit our design for our family totally to God, and he blessed us. Not with pregnancy, but by making it clear we should adopt. A year later, we went to Korea to pick up our son Isaac, who is the light of our lives. A few months after the adoption, we found out we were pregnant with our son Ashton.

People, even Christians, say our pregnancy is a result of the adoption. "You've finally relaxed!" they say. Or, "See, the problem was psychological all along!" We say that God closed our womb for a reason. He had a special design for Isaac and for us.[6]

Children's children are
a crown to the aged,
    and parents are the pride
of their children.

Proverbs 17:6

my sister's wedding

No sooner had I committed myself to being content with my single life than my sister, Linda, got engaged. Our family became consumed by wedding preparations.

Even my vast bridesmaid experience hadn't prepared me for the year of planning that lay ahead, picking out dresses, a reception hall, and a band; hearing about diamonds and china and honeymoon plans; and of course, attending four different wedding showers. To top it all, Linda was getting married on my birthday, the one day I thought would be mine in the midst of The Year of the Wedding.

Envy grew in the pit of my stomach. Linda was only a year older than I. There has always been competition in our relationship, and she had beaten me to the punch on this one. I realized that to be content I needed to put my jealousy aside.

Thankfully, my earlier commitment prepared me for dealing with this new challenge. First, I realized I didn't have to feel shame over being single. If God had a plan for me and I was trusting in his guidance, I didn't have

to worry that my life didn't match up to other's expectations. I didn't have to succumb to their fears that I'd be miserable or incomplete. It was much easier to celebrate Linda's wedding when I felt more secure about myself.

Second, I knew I could be honest with God about what was in my heart. I confessed to him my envy, fear, and sense of failure. He showed me that my feelings were like those of the notorious ugly stepsisters in Cinderella, and he helped me work through those feelings so I could honor my sister. Knowing the God I met that lonely afternoon was still there — the God who loved me, who counted my tears, whom I could trust with all my heart — made all the difference. My struggle with Linda's wedding faded into the background as God began to change my heart.[7]

Endnotes

Chapter 1

1. Kathy Troccoli, "Beauty Never Fades," *Today's Christian Woman* Newsletter
2. Margaret Feinberg, "Makeover Mania," *Today's Christian* (September/October 2004).
3. Karen Lee-Thorp, "Is Beauty the Beast?" *Christianity Today* (July 14, 1997).
4. Kara Davis, M.D., "Weigh to Go!" *Today's Christian Woman* (September/October 2004).
5. Joanna Bloss, "Flex Appeal," *Today's Christian Woman* (September/October 2005).
6. Camerin Courtney, "The Spa Girls," *Today's Christian Woman* (May/June 2005).
7. Renee Ratcliff, "The Weight of my Worth," *Today's Christian Woman* (July/August 2000).
8. Lynn Gauthier, "Confessions of a Former Smoker," *Today's Christian Woman* (November/December 2003).
9. Carol Lee Hall, "Beyond the Blues," *Today's Christian Woman* (July/August 2003).
10. Verla Gillmor, "What Christian Women Don't Tell Their Doctors," *Today's Christian Woman* (November/December 1997).

Chapter 2

1. Joni Eareckson Tada as told to Jane Johnson Struck in "Sweet Surrender," *Today's Christian Woman* (September/October 2004).
2. Katrina Baker, "Just Gotta Have It!" *Today's Christian Woman* (July/August 2004).
3. Joanna Bloss, "Feeling Spiritually Dry?" *Virtue* (December 1999/January 2000).
4. Camerin Courtney, "The Real Facts—and Fun!—of Life," *Today's Christian Woman* (May/June 2004).
5. Rachael Phillips, "Too Busy for God?" *Virtue* (April/May 1999).
6. From "Six ways to squeeze prayer into your busy schedule," *Today's Christian Woman* (September/October 2005).
7. Constance Fink, "You've Got Prayer," *Today's Christian Woman* (July/August 2005).
8. Nancy Ortberg, "No Apology," *Today's Christian Woman* (September/October 2005).
9. Karen Langley, "What's So Amazing About...My Testimony?" *Today's Christian Woman* (May/June 2005).
10. Michelle Steppe (pseudonym), "The Virtue of...Patience," *Virtue* (August/September 1998).
11. Julie-Allyson Ieron, "A New Church Home," *Today's Christian Woman* (July/August 2005).

Chapter 3

1. David Neff, "Take Back Your Sabbath," *Christianity Today* (November 2003).
2. Lauren F. Winner, "Keepin' It Holy," *Christian Parenting Today* (Fall 2005).
3. Lynne M. Baab, "The Gift of Rest," *Today's Christian Woman* (September/October 2005).
4. Deborah R. Simons, "Get Up and Go!" *Today's Christian Woman* (November/December 1998).
5. Debra L. Evans, "Welcome Home, New Mom!" *Christian Parenting Today* (September/October 1998).
6. Mimi Greenwood Knight, "Potty Break," *Today's Christian Woman* (September/October 2005).
7. Ramona Cramer Tucker, "Just Say 'No'!" *Today's Christian Woman* (September/October 2004).
8. Elisha Hodge, "Give Stress a Rest," *Campus Life* (November/December 1998).
9. Camerin Courtney, "What Have You Done for You Lately?" *Today's Christian Woman* (March/April 1999).

Chapter 4

1. Marlee LeDai, "Go Girl!" *Today's Christian Woman* (September/October 2005).
2. "What are your best budget-friendly travel tips?" *Today's Christian Woman* (July/August 2004).
3. Jane Johnson Struck, "Time for a Change?" *Today's Christian Woman* (January/February 1998).
4. Amy Nappa, "That's Entertainment?!" *Today's Christian Woman* (July/August 2002).
5. Theresa Lode, "There's No Place Like Home," *Today's Christian Woman*, (July/August 2003).
6. Jim Killam, "Whatever Happened to Dinner and a Movie?" *Marriage Partnership* (Summer 1998).
7. "What Do You Do for Girlfriend Fun," *Today's Christian Woman* (September/October 2003).
8. Camerin Courtney, "What Have You Done for You Lately?" *Today's Christian Woman* (March/April 1999).

Chapter 5

1. Lynn Bowen Walker, "Coming Clean," *Today's Christian Woman* (March/April 2004).
2. Terry Willits as told to Cindy Crosby, "Why Beauty Matters," *Marriage Partnership* (Winter 2000).
3. Tina Reiman, "Cleaning House," *Virtue* (August/Sep-

tember 1998).

4. Sheila Wright Gregoire, "Real Good Housekeeping," *Marriage Partnership* (Spring 2005).

5. Tammie L. Howell, "My Christmas Tea," *Virtue* (December 1999/January 2000).

6. Elisha Hodge, "Give Stress a Rest," Campus Life (November/December 1998).

7. Annette LaPlaca, "Painless Hospitality," *Marriage Partnership* (Spring 2002).

Chapter 6

1. Thelma Wells, "In God We Trust," *Today's Christian Woman* (January/February 2002).

2. Linda Herbert as told to Lisa Tuttle, "The Day I'll Never Forget," *Today's Christian Woman* (September/October 2004).

3. Phyllis Ten Elshof, "I Was a Victim of Identity Theft," *Today's Christian Woman* (November/December 2004).

4. G. L. Klienhardt, "Is It Sexual Harassment?" *Today's Christian Woman* (November/December 2001).

5. Koren Wetmore, "Wildfire," Today's Christian Woman (September/October 2005).

6. "Stay Safe After Sundown," *Today's Christian Woman* (March/April 2002).

7. Mark Moring, "Separated by War," Marriage Partnership (Summer 2003).

8. Brenda Branson and Don Stewart as told to Corrie Cutrer, "The Silent Epidemic," *Today's Christian Woman* (September/October 2004).

9. Kristina Seleshanko, "We Just Clicked," *Today's Christian Woman* (July/August 2003).

10. John LaRue, ChristianityToday.com

11. Tim Smith, "Creating Refuge," *Christian Parenting Today* (Fall 2005).

12. Laura Polk, "Taking the Lead," *Christian Parenting Today* (Fall 2005).

13. Linda Mintle as told to Jane Johnson Struck, "Risk-Proof Your Child," *Today's Christian Woman* (September/October 2001).

Chapter 7

1. Pam Bianco, "A Mother's Influence," *Virtue* (December 1998/January 1999).

2. Mary Linn McClure, "The Proverbial Grandma," *Virtue* (October/November 1999).

3. Holly Wagner, as told to Camerin Courtney, "Empowering 'God Chicks'," *Today's Christian Woman*

(November/December 2004).

4. Camerin Courtney, "Leaving Legacies," *ChristianSinglesToday.com* (June 25, 2003).

5. Matt Donnelly, *ChristianityToday.com*

6. Jody Veenker, "Are You a Journaling Dropout?" *Today's Christian Woman* (May/June 2004).

7. Linda Kozlowski, "Volunteer Training," *Christian Parenting Today* (Winter 2005).

8. Vanessa Van Cleave, "Lessons in Dying," *Today's Christian Woman*, (July/August 2004).

9. Karl Bruner, as told to Carla Barnhill, "Building a Heritage That Lasts," *Christian Parenting Today* (November/December 2000).

Chapter 8

1. Kelsey Menehan, "Money Madness," *Today's Christian Woman* (March/April 2001).

2. Ibid.

3. Rhonda Rhea, *Today's Christian Woman* (January/February 2003).

4. Katrina Baker, "Surviving the Splurge," *Today's Christian Woman* (January/February 2003).

5. Suzanne Woods Fisher, "Super Savers," *Marriage Partnership* (Summer 2000).

6. Debbie Noffsinger, "Making Allowances," *Christian Parenting Today* (Winter 2003).

7. Cindy Crosby, "Financial Gain, Less Pain," *Marriage Partnership* (Winter 1999).

8. Christin Ditchfield, "How Much Is Enough?" *Today's Christian* (May/June 2005).

Chapter 9

1. Ellen LoDolce, "Kindred Spirits," *Virtue* (June/July 1999).

2. Les and Leslie Parrott, "When You're the Brokenhearted," *ChristianSinglesToday.com* (December 2002).

3. Laurie Jackson, "Laid Off!" *Today's Christian Woman* (July/August 2004).

4. Les and Leslie Parrott, "Newlywed Ambush," *Marriage Partnership* (Spring 1999).

5. Cindy Crosby, "New Girl in Town," *Today's Christian Woman* (January/February 2002).

6. Brian Ray, "Contemplating a Career Change," *FaithInTheWorkplace.com* (October 20, 2004).

7. Cheryl Gochauer, "Stay-at-Home Supermom?" *Today's Christian Woman* (November/December 2001).

8. Angela Williams, "The Work From Home Mom,"

Today's Christian Woman (January/February 2005).
9. Janine Petry, "Unexpectedly Expecting," *Marriage Partnership* (Winter 2000),

Chapter 10

1. Nancy Ortberg, "Hearing God's Call," *Today's Christian Woman* (March/April 2005).
2. Sharon Hersh, "Even Good Women Get Hooked," *Today's Christian Woman*, July/August 1998
3. Mitali Perkins, "The Picture of Greatness," *Virtue* (.June/July 1999).
4. Jane A. G. Kise, "Balancing Act," *Today's Christian Woman* (July/August 2001).
5. Donna R. Carlson, "Working @ Home," *Today's Christian Woman* (May/June 1999).
6. Liz Curtis Higgs, "Who Me, Jealous?" *Today's Christian Woman* (September/October 1997).
7. Mayo Mathers, "Anger Management," *Today's Christian Woman* (January/February 2004).
8. Beth Moore, as told to Jane Johnson Struck, "Beth's Passion," *Today's Christian Woman* (September/October 2005).

Chapter 11

1. Les and Leslie Parrott, "Avoiding Missteps and Misunderstanding," *Marriage Partnership* (Fall 2005).
2. Golden Keyes Parson, "Unforgiven," Marriage Partnership (Summer 2004).
3. Rick Warren, "The Purpose-Driven Marriage," *Marriage Partnership* (Summer 2004).
4. Frederica Mathewes-Green, "Praying for Mr. Right," *Today's Christian* (May/June 2003).
5. Shana Schutte, "Shopping for a Spouse?" *Today's Christian Woman* (September/October 2004).
6. "How do you stay in touch with faraway friends?" *Today's Christian Woman* (July/August 2005).
7. Julie-Allyson Ieron, "My Coworker, My Friend?" *Today's Christian Woman* (May/June 2003).
8. Annette Smith, "Tell It Like It Is," *Today's Christian Woman* (November/December 2002).
9. Sheila Walsh as told to Camerin Courtney, "The Power of Mentoring," *Today's Christian Woman* (July/August 1999).
10. Lauretta Patterson, "Need Hope?" *Virtue* (October/November 1998).

Chapter 12

1. Annette LaPlaca, "Sisters," *Today's Christian Woman* (July/August 1997).
2. Lisa Whelchel, "I'm Such a Worrywart," *Today's Christian Woman* (November/December 2003).
3. Carla Barnhill, "The Wonder of the First Year," *Christian Parenting Today* (November/December 1998).
4. Elizabeth J. Spencer, "Loving Your In-Laws," *Virtue* (October/November 1999).
5. Mary Maslen, "Grasping God," *Today's Christian Woman* (Spring 2004).
6. Marshall Allen, "Married Without Children," *Marriage Partnership* (Fall 2003).
7. Lori Smith, "Single Minded," *Today's Christian Woman* (March/April 2000).

At Inspirio, we would love to hear your stories and your feedback. Please send your comments to us by way of email icares@zondervan.com or to the address below:

inspirio

Attn: Inspirio Cares
5300 Patterson Avenue SE
Grand Rapids, MI 49530

If you would like further information about Inspirio and the products we create, please visit us at:
www.inspiriogifts.com

Thank you and God bless!